A Bible Believer's Bible Summary

by Eric Neumann

Copyright 2015

Copyright Notice

The author hereby grants permission for any and all material within this book to be reproduced free of any fees to the author, provided that said materials are not sold for a profit.

Quotations

The only material quoted in this book is the Word of God in the King James Version. No commentaries or scholars are quoted, because God's Word is important, not man's word. As such, I encourage all readers to be good Bereans by searching the scriptures to see if what I have said is true (Acts 17:11). It is okay if you do not agree with what I say, but it is not okay if your disagreement is not based upon the Word of God in its proper context, which involves "rightly dividing the Word of Truth" (II Timothy 2:15).

Goal

The goal of this book is to cast "down imaginations, and every high thing that exalteth itself against the knowledge of God and [bring] into captivity every thought to the obedience of Christ" (II Corinthians 10:5) so that members of the body of Christ may "come unto the knowledge of the truth" (I Timothy 2:4).

Contact the author

Therefore, the author encourages any disagreements be brought to his attention so that future versions can be changed if deemed necessary.

You may e-mail the author at Bibledivider@gmail.com.

Other books by the author may be purchased by going to http://www.amazon.com/author/bibledivider.

Section I.

A detailed summary of the Bible in book order

Introduction

This section of this book gives a summary of the entire Bible in story format by going in book order, which shows that God put the books of the Bible in the order that He did for a reason. Therefore, much more benefit will come from reading the Bible in this order than by trying to figure out a chronological order and following that. To follow the book order, each book's name is in bold to show where the summary of that book starts.

In the beginning, God creates humans and gives them free will so they have the option to either have faith in Him or not. Those, with faith in Him, will be like Him (I John 3:2) and will live with Him for ever (Ephesians 1:10-12). Those, without faith in Him, will be cast into the lake of fire to burn for ever (Isaiah 66:24). God knew, in advance, that Lucifer would rebel against Him, become Satan, and want to take God's position as possessor of heaven and earth (Isaiah 14:12-14), and God made the lake of fire, specifically for the devil and his angels (Matthew 25:41). Hell was not made for man, because God is "not willing that any should perish, but that all should come to repentance" (II Peter 3:9). Therefore, God does not send people to hell. Rather, He sent His Son to die for man (Romans 5:8). Nevertheless, because of man's unbelief, hell has had to enlarge itself to accommodate unbelieving man (Isaiah 5:14).

Bible summary

The Bible starts with the book of **Genesis**. The first thing we are told is that God created the heaven and the earth (Genesis 1:1), and the focus is immediately placed on the earth (Genesis 1:2). God gives man dominion over the earth (Psalm 8:5-8), and Lucifer rebels against God, setting his sight on taking dominion over the earth away from man (Ezekiel 28:15-18; Isaiah 14:12-14).

Satan attacks mankind through the woman (Eve), and the man (Adam) sins against God by eating of the tree of the knowledge of good and evil, breaking God's command (Genesis 3:1-6). Immediately, we see them come up with their own way to be okay in God's eyes by sewing fig leaves together to cover their nakedness (Genesis 3:7), since they have now lost their clothing of light (Genesis 1:27; Psalm 104:1-2). The fig leaves represent man's way of getting back to God, which is called religion. Because man's way never works, God provides His covering for man, so that he might be reconciled back to God, by providing animal sacrifices and making coats of animal skins to hide their sin from God (Genesis 3:21).

However, religion continues, and it gets worse to the point that Adam's son, Cain, kills his other son, Abel, because God accepted Abel's sacrifice of faith, but He did not accept Cain's sacrifice of religion (Genesis 4:1-8). As time goes on, we do see some men worship the Lord (Genesis 4:26), but, as a whole, man gets more steeped in his own ways to the point, that, just 10 generations after Adam, in the days of Noah, every thought of man is only evil continually (Genesis 6:5). Man is so wicked that even devils have sex with women and create superhuman creatures (Genesis 6:1-4).

The reason for the superhuman creatures is because, even though Satan got dominion of the earth from man (Adam), when that happened, God immediately made the promise that, the woman, through whom Satan got man to sin, would have a seed to redeem man so that God could give dominion of the earth back over to man (Genesis 3:15). Thus, dominion is lost and gained through the woman. That seed of the woman, as scripture later reveals, turns out to be the Lord Jesus Christ, but He will not show up on earth for another 4,000 years. The Bible records attack after attack by Satan on the seed of the woman, culminating in killing the Lord Jesus Christ on a cross. The attack in Genesis 6 is Satan's effort to pollute the seed line of the woman through devils having sex with women.

To prevent Satan's plan from working, God creates a worldwide flood that destroys all of mankind, except for Noah and his family (Genesis 6-8). So, man is saved, and God starts mankind all over again with Noah (Genesis 9:1). 10 generations from Noah's son, Shem, Abram is born. Just like the 10 generations from Adam to Noah, the 10 generations from Shem to Abram show a progressive wickedness in man to the point that man builds a tower to make a name for himself so that he may be God himself (Genesis 11:3-4). God concludes that man will succeed in his plan, if God does not stop him. Therefore, God divides united men into nations and language groups so that they cannot all conspire together to overthrow God and make Satan their God (Genesis 11:5-9). Romans 1:28-32 says that this event is God giving man over to a reprobate mind, allowing man to do whatever he wants to do, leading him ultimately to receive the wrath of God in an eternal lake of fire (Romans 1:18).

However, God does not give up on ALL of mankind. He will still be faithful to His promise to use the seed of the woman to reconcile man back to God. Therefore, just like God used one man—Noah—to continue the seed line, God uses one man—Abram—whom He later renames Abraham, through whom the seed line will continue (Genesis 12:7). It is important to note that God did not choose Abram because he was a godly man. In fact, Joshua 24:2 states that Abram's father, Terah, served other gods. Rather, Abram was chosen because he would simply believe the promises God would make to him (Genesis 15:1-6). Hebrews 11:6 says that it is impossible to please God without faith. Thus, eternal life, regardless of when you live, is not based upon your good works but upon believing what God has told you to believe (Romans 3:28).

We also need to note that, since God created nationalism, God would make a great nation of Abram. We learn later that this nation is called Israel, which is the name that God gave to Abram's grandson, Jacob

(Genesis 32:28). It is through the nation of Israel that God will reconcile all nations of the earth back to Himself (Genesis 12:1-3; Exodus 19:5-6). This promise to Abram, found in Genesis 12:1-3, is why Israel is focused on throughout the Old Testament.

The reason God chose Israel is because they would be a nation of faith. Abraham's wife, Sarah, could not bear children (Genesis 16:1-2). God then waited until Abraham was past being able to have children before He gave Abraham the promised child (Hebrews 11:11-12). That way, the child who was born, Isaac, came from the Lord, rather than from man (Genesis 21:1-2). Isaac was the child of faith in Eve's line (Genesis 3:15), as well, meaning the seed of the woman comes through Israel. Isaac marries Rebekah, who is also barren. It is only by Isaac's praying to the Lord that Rebekah has children (Genesis 25:21). She has twin sons—Esau and Jacob. Traditionally, the firstborn son receives the blessing and continues the seed line. However, this is God's nation of faith—not man's nation of religion or tradition. Therefore, God declares that "the elder shall serve the younger" (Genesis 25:23). God continues the seed line through the younger, Jacob, not because of his good works, but because of his faith in God.

It is also important to recognize that God actually made 2 covenants with Abram for 2, different groups of people coming out of him. The first covenant is that Abraham is justified by faith alone (Romans 3:28) in God's promise to make his seed as numerous as the stars in heaven (Genesis 15:5-6). This covenant was made unconditionally by God and before God began the nation of Israel (Genesis 15:17). The recognition of this covenant will become vitally important once we get to Romans (Romans 4:1-10), because God keeps it a secret until then that He did, in fact, make 2, distinct covenants with Abraham. After making this unconditional covenant with Abraham, God begins the nation of Israel with a conditional covenant of circumcision (Genesis 17:6-14), so that Israel is justified by faith plus works (James 2:24).

Since Genesis' focus is on the earth (Genesis 1:2), God only talks about this second covenant for now. Israel, Abraham's grandson, has 12 sons, through his two wives and two concubines. Again, we see that God's choice is not the firstborn, Reuben, because of his lack of faith in God (Genesis 49:3-4). God builds up the nation of Israel through Joseph, Israel's eleventhborn son (Genesis 29:31 – 30:24), who is the best type of the Lord Jesus Christ found in scripture. However, God actually continues the seed of the woman through Judah, Israel's fourthborn son (Matthew 1:2-3), and it is the secondborn son, two generations later (Genesis 38:28-30), that continues the seed line (Matthew 1:3). Again, this shows that Israel is a nation of faith, making it God's nation, rather than man's nation of religion or tradition. God uses Joseph to move Israel to Egypt, at which time, there are 70 people in Israel's party (Genesis 46:27).

Israel stays in Egypt for approximately 400 years. This time is needed for the iniquity of the Promised Land's inhabitants to reach the point where they are so evil that they will not be saved (Genesis 15:13-16). The 400 years also gives Israel time to grow into a nation, which goes from 70 total people to 603,355 male soldiers (Numbers 1:45-46), which means that there were easily over 2 million Israelites at the time. In fact, Israel outgrows Egypt, even though they were in bondage to Egypt (Exodus 1:9). These 400 years take place between the books of Genesis and **Exodus**. During this time, Israel is supposed to be an example of faith in God to the Egyptians around them. Instead, they assimilate into the Egyptian culture, worshipping and serving their gods.

When the time comes for Israel to enter the Promised Land, God calls Moses to lead Israel into the wilderness, abandoning their Egyptian gods and sacrificing to the Lord God instead (Exodus 5:3). Just like God started the nation of Israel with the faith of Abram, God starts

Israel's "Exodus" from Egypt with the faith of Moses' parents in preserving him, against the king's commandment (Hebrews 11:23), while the king's commandment to destroy all Jewish males at birth (Exodus 1:15-16) was yet another attack by Satan on the seed of the woman (Genesis 3:15).

When the time has come for God to lead Israel out of Egypt, God raises up Moses and sends ten plagues upon Egypt, so that Israel will know that the Lord God is the only true God and so the rest of the world will know it, too. Israel's "Exodus" from Egypt culminates in God parting the Red Sea, with Israel walking through on dry land and Pharaoh and his army drowning to death (Exodus 14:26-31). God is ready to bring Israel into the Promised Land. All they have to do is have faith in God to bring them there. Their period of testing would be 40 days in the wilderness with no food or water (Matthew 4:1-2). If they learn to live by faith, rather than by bread alone (Matthew 4:4), they will take possession of the land forever. Unfortunately, they only lasted 3 days before they started complaining (Exodus 15:22-24). Thus, their lack of faith meant that generation would not enter the Promised Land (Numbers 14:34-35).

All men know that there is a God and that He is worthy of our worship (Romans 1:19-20). Israel had the further proof of God through all the miracles He did, and they still did not believe. Therefore, to bring them to a place of belief, God had to give them a law, in addition to the law of the conscience written on their hearts (Romans 2:14-15). Therefore, in Exodus 20, Moses met with the Lord, where God gave Israel the written law, so that they may trust in Him. Not long afterward, God sent spies into the land of Canaan, i.e., the Promised Land, to see if Israel now had faith in God to give them the land, and they did not. Therefore, instead of spending 40 days in the wilderness, they would now spend 40 years, and, out of the millions of Israelites in the wilderness, only Joshua and Caleb, the 2 spies who had faith in God, would actually enter the Promised Land. The rest of Israel would die in the wilderness (Numbers 14:29-34).

Israel was God's firstborn (Exodus 4:22). God chose them as "a special people unto Himself, above all people that are upon the face of the earth" (Deuteronomy 7:6). They were then to be a kingdom of priests to the nations (Exodus 19:5-6) so that God will bless all nations through them (Genesis 12:3). However, with Israel in unbelief, God has to create a mediator and a buffer zone between Himself and Israel.

When Moses came down from the mount after receiving God's law for Israel and found them worshipping a golden calf, it was the Levites who stood up and agreed to kill those in Israel, who led them into idolatry, so as to keep God's wrath from killing all of Israel (Exodus 32:25-28). From then on, the Levites would be the priestly tribe of Israel, being the mediators between God and Israel so that God's wrath would be kept from Israel. To keep Israel from being killed, God's presence within Israel is confined within a temple. A temple cannot contain God (I Kings 8:27), but it can corral God's wrath. So, in Exodus 28-30, we are given details of how the Levitical priests are consecrated unto the Lord. Then, in Exodus 25-27 and 36-40, detailed instructions are given for building God's tabernacle and all of its components. It is important to note that God promises that all of Israel, not just the Levites, will be a kingdom of priests to reconcile the Gentiles back to Himself (Exodus 19:5-6), and, thus, reclaim the earth for Himself through Israel. The book of Exodus concludes with the glory of the Lord safely contained within the tabernacle (Exodus 40:35), so that God can lead an unbelieving Israel in the wilderness for 40 years without killing them. It is not that God wants to destroy them, but, in order to remain a holy God, He cannot be contaminated by sin (Leviticus 11:44-45).

Thus, the book of **Leviticus** shows how a holy God can be the God of Israel, even when Israel is unholy herself.

First, the holy, Levitical priesthood is created, which involves various cleansings, garments, and ceremonies necessary for the priests to be clean enough to meet with a holy God. Then, the children of Israel must bring certain sacrifices to God via the priests, in order for God to be pleased with them. These sacrifices are detailed in Leviticus 1-7. Chapter 8 shows how the priests are to be consecrated to God themselves. Chapter 10 shows the danger of coming to God without being properly cleansed. Then, chapters 11-27 give the various rules that God set up to set Israel apart as a holy, sanctified people for God. People look at these laws as strange, such as not being able to have their cattle breed with a different kind of cattle (19:19), not rounding the corners of their beards in shaving (19:27), or not eating certain animals (11), but they were all laws given to separate Israel out as God's people and for them to learn the greater spiritual truth of the necessity of having faith in what God tells them. A very important chapter in Leviticus is chapter 26, because it sets out the five cycles of chastisement that Israel will receive from God during their future history of disobedience in order for Israel to come finally to the place of having faith in what God has told them. We can see Israel go through these cycles as we read through the Bible.

The book of **Numbers** gets its name from the census of 603,550 fighting men led out of Egypt at the beginning of the book (Numbers 1:46), and the 601,730 fighting men of the next generation of Israelites at the end of the 40 years in the wilderness, who actually go into the Promised Land toward the end of the book (Numbers 26:51). It shows that God will not fulfill His promises to Israel when they do not believe what He has told them, as the size of Israel remains stagnant during the 40 years in the wilderness, as God purges out a generation steeped in Egyptian idolatry. The purging is seen in the events mentioned in the book, such as the "very great plague" of 11:33, and the 15,000 or so killed in the rebellion of Korah (16:31-35, 49), while God separates out those in Israel, with faith in Him, as seen in the

Nazarite vow (Numbers 6) and the water of separation (Numbers 19).

With the 40 years in the wilderness drawing to a conclusion, the book of **Deuteronomy** gives the second reading of the law. Moses had to give the law to Israel again to make sure the generation of Jews entering the Promised Land has the opportunity to be God's holy people, since the generation of unbelieving Jews would not have passed God's law down to their children. Thus, we see Moses speaking the law in the eleventh month of the 40th year that Israel is in the wilderness (Deuteronomy 1:3), and Moses commands them to teach the law to the generations that will follow them (6:6-7, 11:18-21), so that future generations will fully possess the Promised Land. The book warns them of the curses they will receive if they disobey the law (27:14-26; 28:15-68), as well as the blessings they will receive if they obey it (28:1-14).

Thus, God gives Israel the opportunity to be His children and prosper in the land. However, since God knows the future, He also prophesies of their future punishment for disobedience, even to the point of telling them that He will raise up the Israel of God (Galatians 6:16) from among them and give them the Promised Land, over the apostate nation of Israel (32:21; Matthew 21:43). Thus, both death and life are set before them (30:19). The book ends with Moses' death (34:5) and with Joshua taking over to lead Israel into the Promised Land (34:9).

The book of **Joshua** shows the glory days of Israel. God leads Israel into the Promised Land under Joshua, and Israel begins utterly destroying the Canaanites there, as God commanded them to do. The reason they are to destroy the Canaanites is because of their great wickedness, made possible by "the Canaanite" (Genesis 12:6), Satan himself, who immediately went into the land, once God made the promise to Abram to give him the land, as yet another attack on the seed of the woman. We do see a few problems in the book of Joshua with Achan taking possessions for himself (Joshua 7:1) and Israel making a covenant with the Gibeonites, who they should have destroyed instead (Joshua 9:14-15). However, other than these problems, Israel defeats their enemies and takes possession of the land of Canaan (Joshua 14-21). However, by the time Joshua is about to die, there is still a lot of land left for Israel to take over in Canaan (Joshua 13:1). Before he dies, Joshua gives Israel their options, as did Moses, and Israel says they will serve the Lord (Joshua 24:21). However, when we read Judges, we find that they did not keep their promise for long.

The book of **Judges** begins with Israel looking directly to God to lead them in conquering the rest of the Promised Land (Judges 1:1-2). However, it is not long before they begin trusting in riches, rather than in God. Therefore, they begin to make the Canaanites their servants, so that they can get tribute money from them, rather than utterly destroying them as God had commanded (Judges 1:28-36). The Lord God was to be Israel's ruler, but, with the death of Joshua and that generation, Israel fell into idolatry (Judges 2:10-13). Israel goes from destroying Canaan, to subduing Canaan, to being destroyed by Canaan, thanks to their sinful slide from serving the Lord, to desiring material riches, to serving other gods. Judges covers over 300 years of Israel's history, and Judges 2:14-19 gives a summary of this period. First, God delivers Israel into the hands of the enemy because Israel is rebelling against God. Second, Israel asks for God's help, and He sends a "judge" to deliver them from their enemy. Third, once the judge dies, Israel goes back into idolatry worse than before. These three steps repeat themselves over this 300-year period.

Because Israel gets more and more involved in idolatry as time goes on, the judges God sends to deliver Israel have less and less faith in God. In Judges 4, Israel is shamed by having a woman deliverer, because she appears to be the only one with faith. In Judges 6, Gideon fights tooth and nail with God before he finally agrees to deliver Israel. In Judges 14-17, God gives Samson superhuman strength, and he still wastes his life, only destroying God's enemies for fleshly reasons. He finally has faith in God in the end, but the deliverance he brings costs him his life. Therefore, by the time we get to the end of Judges, Israel is just as wicked as Sodom and Gomorrah, as seen by comparing Judges 19 with Genesis 19. The book of Judges concludes with the statement that, "every man did that which was right in his own eyes" (Judges 21:25).

But, all is not lost. There is still a faithful remnant in Israel, as seen in the book of **Ruth**. Ruth reminds us of God's plan of reconciling the earth back to Himself through the seed of the woman (Genesis 3:15) and Israel (Exodus 19:5-6). Both come together in the Lord Jesus Christ, as typified by Boaz, the kinsmen redeemer, who saves Ruth, a Gentile by birth, but a Jew by marriage, just like saved Israel will come out of the heathen and marry the Lord Jesus Christ in God's eternal kingdom on earth.

The encouraging story of Ruth and Boaz is needed because Israel enters a new phase of even greater idolatry with the book of **I Samuel**. There, God's special people, above all the nations of the earth (Deuteronomy 7:6), become just like the nations of the earth, by rejecting God as their king, wanting a human king to rule over them, just like other nations (I Samuel 8:5-7).

Because God is no longer their king, God raises up a new group of people, called prophets. They will speak God's judgment to Israel, do extreme things to get Israel's attention, and perform miracles to show that God is with them so that a believing remnant will come out of Israel and follow God's law covenant with them, rather than participating in the idolatry of the nation as a whole.

The next 600 years covers this period of time of the Jews' kings and God's prophets, and the history of this time is found in I Samuel – II Kings. Now, Abraham and Moses were prophets of God, in the sense that they spoke for the Lord, but the new prophets God is now calling are to be the leaders, not of the entire nation of Israel, but of a believing remnant to come out of the apostate nation of Israel and trust in the Lord God of Israel. Samuel was the first to be called a prophet in this new capacity, and, because it was new, God had to call him four times before he even realized it was God speaking to him (I Samuel 3).

When Israel asks for a king to rule over them, God gives them their choice, Saul (I Samuel 10-11), so that they may see the error of their ways. God then raises up his choice, David, and anoints him as His king over Israel (I Samuel 16:13), even though it is not until after Saul's death, some 20 years later, that all of Israel acknowledges David as their king (**II Samuel** 2:4, 3:21). As such, Saul is a type of the Antichrist, and David is a type of the Christ. Jews, siding with Saul, are a type of apostate Israel, who will not make it into God's eternal kingdom on earth. Jews, siding with David, are a type of the believing remnant of Israel, who will be in the kingdom. Since David is a type of Christ, the rest of II Samuel shows him winning many battles and becoming the dominant nation of the world.

The book of **I Kings** starts with David's death (I Kings 2:10), and his son, Solomon, being anointed king (I Kings 1:39). Israel's kingdom reaches its peak under Solomon, as he builds the house of the Lord (I Kings 6), but it is the height of man, not of God, that is reached during Solomon's time, as evidenced by the 666 talents of gold he received in tribute in a year (I Kings 10:14). This makes Solomon a type of the Antichrist, since the number of his name will be 666 (Revelation 13:18), the height of man. Solomon leads Israel back into sin, having 700 wives and 300 concubines, who turn him away from God (I Kings 11:1-8). Knowing that things will only get worse from here on out, God divides Israel into two kingdoms—Israel and Judah (I Kings 11:31-36). God, essentially, sets aside all of Israel, except for the one tribe of Judah, because Judah is where Jerusalem is, from where God's earthly kingdom will be centered for all eternity (Isaiah 2:1-3). It is no coincidence, then, that Jesus came from the tribe of Judah (Revelation 5:5). Thus, the seed of the woman has been narrowed from the world to the nation of Israel to the tribe of Judah.

The rest of I Kings - **II Kings** is Israel's/Judah's progressive slide into idolatry under a series of man's kings, culminating in Israel going into Gentile captivity, never to be their own sovereign nation again until Jesus sets up God's kingdom at His second coming (Daniel 2:36-45). Every, single king in Israel, from here on out, is evil, while almost all of the kings in Judah are evil. The reason all of Israel's kings are evil is that God's temple is in Jerusalem, which is in Judah. To keep the tribes of Israel from leaving Israel and going to Judah, the first king of Israel in the divided kingdom, Jeroboam, sets up idols and false temples in Israel (I Kings 12:26-33), and Israel follows them from then on. The capital city in Israel is Samaria, and, in Jesus' day, the Jews in Jerusalem consider the Samaritans worse than the Gentiles.

During the time of kings in Israel, Ahab stands out as a very evil king in Israel (I Kings 16:30), who leads Israel into full-blown Baal worship, due to his pagan wife, Jezebel (I Kings 16:31-33). God counteracts the strong influence of Baal worship in Israel by empowering the prophet, Elijah, to do great miracles for God, followed by Elisha, who does twice the miracles that Elijah did, since he received a double portion. Both Israel and Judah go into captivity for 70 years. First, Israel goes into Assyrian captivity (II Kings 17:6), around 610 BC. Then, Judah goes into Babylonian captivity (II Kings 24:10-16), around 490 BC. We also see Satan make another attack on the seed of the woman, and he comes very close to succeeding. However, Jehosheba saves the remaining seed, Joash, alive to sit as the king of Judah at the age of seven (II Kings 11:1-3, 12:1).

The books of **I and II Chronicles** go back and cover the period of the kings from a spiritual perspective. I Chronicles is interested in chronicling the important names, so far, in God's history of His people. Chronicles' history starts with Adam (I Chronicles 1:1) and quickly gets to Abraham (I Chronicles 1:27). I Chronicles 2-9 records names in Israel, starting from the twelve tribes, and ending in Saul's line. Chapter 10 is spent showing Saul's death, and 11:1 has David being crowned king. Before we get out of chapter 11, we are given the names of David's mighty men. Finally, names related to temple work are given in I Chronicles 23-27.

The four books of the kings, i.e., I Samuel – II Kings, record Israel's history, more from man's perspective, while the Chronicles record the history of God's people from God's perspective. There are over 100 parallel passages between the four books of the kings and the Chronicles, but the details given are different, due to their different focus. For example, at Saul's death, I Chronicles 10:13-14 mentions that he died for his sin, while I Samuel 31 does not tell why Saul was killed. Another example is that II Samuel 24:1 says that the Lord moved David to number Israel and Judah, which was against God's command, while I Chronicles 21:1 tells us that it was really Satan who provoked David to number Israel. Thus, Satan tempted David in Chronicles, but, in II Samuel, the Lord is said to have done it indirectly by allowing Satan to tempt David. As such, Chronicles provides valuable information of the spirit behind Israel's history and also show the important events, from God's perspective, that are harder to see in the four books of the kings. Therefore, Chronicles' information compliments, rather than contradicts, the four books of the kings. Since the Chronicles concentrate on God's people, when the kingdom is divided, the Chronicles focus only on Judah, since that is the tribe God reserved for Himself at that time, and they end with Judah in Babylonian captivity (II Chronicles 36:14-21).

The first 2 ½ verses of the book of **Ezra** are exactly the same as the last two verses of II Chronicles, showing that Ezra is a continuation of Judah's history. Ezra shows Judah coming back to Jerusalem, from her 70 years in Babylonian captivity, and rebuilding God's house (Ezra 1:2). It also shows Judah confessing her sins (Ezra 9). (Judah's 70 years of Babylonian captivity is a type of the 7 years of tribulation that Israel will go through in Babylon, that is detailed in the book of the Revelation.)

The book of **Nehemiah** also shows Judah coming back to Jerusalem from Babylonian captivity, but it is concerned with the rebuilding of the city (Nehemiah 2:5). With both temple and city being in place, Nehemiah concludes with Israel putting themselves back under the law covenant God made with Israel (Nehemiah 9:38) and reforming themselves to obey its provisions (Nehemiah 13). Both Ezra and Nehemiah end around 400 BC and are the last recorded history books in the Old Testament.

We should also note that Ezra and Nehemiah are types of how the Lord Jesus Christ will come, at the end of the tribulation period, cleanse believing Israel (Ezekiel 36:25), bring them into the Promised Land (Isaiah 40:9-11), put His Spirit within them, and cause them to obey the provisions of His covenant with them (Ezekiel 36:26-27).

The book of **Esther** gives a physical example of God's spiritual deliverance of Israel from Satan, and Job shows the physical trials Israel must go through before they will accept God's spiritual deliverance of them from Satan.

Esther is the only book of the Bible that never mentions God, yet it shows how the Lord Jesus Christ delivers Judah from being Satan's lawful captive (Isaiah 49:24-25). Judah is in captivity. God raises up a Jew, Esther, to be queen (Esther 2:17). A Gentile, Haman, convinces the king to have all Jews killed (Esther 3:13). Mordecai, a Jew, prays for deliverance (Esther 4:1-3). Esther intercedes to the king for the Jews (Esther 7:3-4). Haman is killed (Esther 7:10), and a commandment is issued, allowing the Jews to defend themselves on the day they were to be killed (Esther 8:11-13). On the day they were to be killed, "no man could withstand them" (the Jews) (Esther 9:2).

Now, let's interpret the typology. Because they have broken God's law covenant with them, Israel is Satan's lawful captive (Isaiah 49:24-25), just like Judah is in captivity in the days of Esther. Satan wants to kill all of God's people, just like Haman wanted all of the Jews to be killed. The believing remnant prays for God's deliverance, just like Mordecai did. The Lord Jesus Christ promises to redeem Judah from the one stronger than them, i.e., Satan (Jeremiah 31:10-11). He does so as the seed of the woman (Genesis 3:15). He intercedes to the Father for Israel, just like the woman, Esther, interceded to the king for deliverance. The Lord Jesus Christ comes and kills the Antichrist, just like Haman was killed. In Satan's final battle with the Lord Jesus Christ and His saints, Satan is killed, just like the Jews survive the day they were supposed to be killed in Esther's day. Thus, Esther is a story of Israel's physical deliverance to point them to the spiritual deliverance that the seed of the woman will give them, bringing them into God's eternal kingdom on earth.

The Jews readily saw the physical deliverance they needed in Esther's day. However, when Jesus comes, they fail to see the spiritual deliverance they need. In order for them to see this and trust in God and the Lord Jesus Christ to save them, they must go through the seven-year tribulation period. The book of **Job** is a type of this. Therefore, we can see why Job is placed in the Bible where it is, even though it was the first book of the Bible written.

Satan claims that Job will deny God (1:9-11; 2:4-6) if he loses his health, wealth, and family. Those things are taken away from him, except for his wife, who he rejects (1:14-19; 2:7-9). He then has three "friends," who are against him (4-31). Finally, a fourth friend and God show him the truth (32-41), he repents from his self righteousness and trusts in God's righteousness to save him (42:1-6). Then, God restores him, giving him double what he had before this all started (42:10-17).

Similarly, Satan claims that Israel belongs to him. During the tribulation period, Satan takes away the believing remnant of Israel's health, wealth, and family (Revelation 13:17; Matthew 10:21-22), except for their spiritual wife or religion (Revelation 17:3-6; Matthew 17:20-21), which they reject. Their friends, i.e., apostate Israel, are against them. Finally, God shows them the truth through the two witnesses (Revelation 11:3) and the little flock (Matthew 25:6). They repent from their self righteousness and trust in God's righteousness (Matthew 25:7). Then, God restores them, giving them an hundredfold in the kingdom (Matthew 19:29).

The book of **Psalms** shows the history of man on the earth from beginning to end. It is divided into five books to correspond with Genesis – Deuteronomy. Psalms 1-41 is the Genesis book, showing man and his fall and how man ultimately overcomes Satan through the man, Christ Jesus. Psalms 42-72 is the Exodus book, showing God's nation, Israel, and their rebellion. Israel ultimately overcomes through their Redeemer, the Lord Jesus Christ. Psalms 73-89 is the Leviticus book, showing God's temple on the earth. This temple is desecrated by Israel, but it is ultimately made holy by the Lord Jesus Christ. Psalms 90-106 is the Numbers book, showing how Israel and the nations lose the earth to Satan, but it is regained by the Lord Jesus Christ. Finally, Psalms 107-150 shows God and His Word delivering and sustaining the world, culminating in the praise of the Lord by the whole earth for all eternity in Psalms 145-150. Thus, Psalms gives Israel a complete picture of mankind from beginning to end, showing them that the only way they will live for eternity on the earth is by aligning themselves with God and His Word.

The book of **Proverbs** shows Israel the two women, competing for their affections throughout their entire history and ultimately in the tribulation period. The woman they chose determines where they will spend eternity. The first woman is God's wisdom, which is found in God's law covenant with Israel. If Israel believes God's Word to them, they will have righteousness (Proverbs 2:1-9). However, the prevalent "woman" in Israel is the Jewish religion, which is at its worst under the Antichrist in the tribulation period. Because the Jewish religion, Babylon, is so enticing to the flesh, she is described as "subtil of heart ..., stubborn ..., came...diligently to seek thy face ..., and with her much fair speech she caused him to yield, with the flattering of her lips she forced him" (Proverbs 7:10,11,15,21). By contrast, to believe God, Israel must seek out God's wisdom and mine it out as hidden treasure (Proverbs 2:4). Thus, Proverbs is given so that Israel may understand this and believe God and His law covenant with them, even though most of Israel rejects it. (A practical application for us today is that we should seek out the truth of God's Word and believe it, even though most Christians will follow the "Christian" religion instead.)

The book of **Ecclesiastes** is written by Solomon and is concerning wisdom, just like Proverbs is. The difference is that, while Proverbs shows the difference between God's wisdom and the Jewish religious system, Ecclesiastes shows the foolishness of pursuing the things of this world. Solomon had great wisdom, riches, and power, which meant, if anyone could find value in the things of this world, he could. But, his conclusion was, "vanity of vanities; all is vanity" (Ecclesiastes 1:2). Therefore, when Israel is in the tribulation period and is offered great riches and power if they align themselves with the Antichrist, they need to learn the lesson of the preacher that all worldly pursuits are vanity. Israel needs to reject the things offered to them by the Antichrist and trust in the things God offers them through His law covenant with them. "Fear God, and keep His commandments: for this is the whole duty of man" (Ecclesiastes 12:13).

Ultimately, the true Israel of God, comprised of physical Jews, but not all physical Jews, will choose to obey God's commandments, because of their love for their Christ. This love relationship between the Lord Jesus Christ and Israel, His bride, is shown in the book of the **Song of Solomon**. The Lord Jesus Christ and Israel are apart for most of the book because Jesus Christ had not yet come when it was written, and He has only come once since. However, His second coming will involve His marrying Israel (Isaiah 62:4; Revelation 21:2-3) and being with her forever. Song of Solomon is designed to give Israel faith that her Bridegroom will come and marry her when "His wife hath made herself ready" (Revelation 19:7), which is at the end of the tribulation period.

After the bad history of Israel from Exodus through Nehemiah, the books of Esther through Song of Solomon come along to show that God, through the Lord Jesus Christ, will be faithful to redeem the earth through the seed of the woman through Israel. The Jews, who will be part of Israel's bride, will be those, who believe in God's law covenant with Israel to bring them into the kingdom by faith.

Isaiah – Malachi conclude the Old Testament and are the books of Israel's written prophets. God began the era of using prophets to reach Israel with Samuel, around 1,060 BC, which is about the time when Israel rejected God as their king. Samuel, Elijah, and Elisha are prolific prophets of Israel, which continue for about 300 years. Then, about 100 years later, God begins using the written prophets of Isaiah – Malachi, which are all written between 700 and 400 BC. Think of Israel as a bad employee, who is too well loved by the employer to ever be fired. As a bad employee, they are given verbal warnings for 300 years, through Samuel, Elijah, and Elisha. Since they do not heed the verbal warnings, written reprimands are needed, which are given in Isaiah through Malachi for another 300-year period. Because Judah is primarily God's people, most of these written prophets are to Judah. However, some are also to Israel. These written prophets are called to do some unusual things, at times, to get Israel's attention. Most of these writings are just before Judah and Israel go into captivity, but some are also written during and after the captivity periods.

The book of **Isaiah** is at the beginning of the prophetic section of the Old Testament, which goes all the way through Malachi. He writes earlier than most prophets and is the second longest book in the entire Bible in terms of number of chapters. Isaiah's prophecy is to Judah. Judah is so steeped in sin and idolatry by this point that God actually calls them Sodom and Gomorrah (1:10), which God destroyed in Genesis 19. Isaiah speaks for the Lord to Judah for them to repent (change their mind) and put themselves back under God's law covenant with Israel so that they will not be destroyed, like Sodom and Gomorrah were.

Judah is so steeped in their idolatry that Isaiah prophesies naked for three years just to get their attention (20:2-4). Isaiah promises the Messiah, the seed of the woman, to come, save them from their sins, and bring them into God's kingdom on earth (7:14, 9:6-7, 2:3). Chapters 13-24 show God's judgment of the various nations, which shows that God does have the power to execute judgment, and He will do so on Judah, as well, if they do not abandon their own self righteousness (64:6).

Judah receives a taste of this judgment in chapter 36, when Assyria comes and takes the defenced cities of Judah (36:1). They will not go into captivity now, but they will soon, if they do not repent (change their mind). The good news is that the Messiah will save those in Judah, who place their faith in God's law covenant with them. We see this salvation in chapters 40-66, especially in chapters 52-53, where the Christ is wounded for Judah's transgressions, bruised for their iniquities, and

Judah is healed by His stripes (53:5). Thus, in God's kingdom on earth, Israel finally fulfills their calling to be a kingdom of priests to the Gentiles to reconcile the earth back to God (61:6). God creates new heavens and a new earth (65:17). The book of Isaiah ends with all those, with faith in what God told them, being in God's eternal kingdom on earth, while unbelievers burn forever in the lake of fire (66:22-24).

It should be noted that Isaiah has 66 chapters, as the Bible has 66 books, and each chapter relates to its book in the same order the Bible is given in. For example, the 40th book of the Bible is Matthew, and "the voice of him that crieth in the wilderness" (40:3), i.e., John the Baptist, is mentioned in Isaiah 40. Such a marked contrast is seen between the first 39 chapters of Isaiah and the last 27 chapters of Isaiah, that most cemetery (seminary) students are taught that there were two people named "Isaiah," each one writing their section of the book. However, Bible believers understand that the marked contrast between the two sections is due to the marked contrast seen between the Old and New Testaments, due to the coming of the Messiah to begin the New Testament. Isaiah starts with Israel lost and ends with them in the kingdom, just like Genesis shows man lost and Revelation shows Israel in the kingdom.

Jeremiah's prophecy is to Judah and occurs before and at the beginning of Judah's 70 years in Babylonian captivity. Since Jeremiah is after Isaiah, Judah is in even greater rebellion than they were at the time of Isaiah's prophecy. They serve the queen of heaven (7:18-20), who is known as the perpetual virgin Mary in today's Catholic church. They are so far removed from serving God that God tells Jeremiah not to pray for Judah, because He will not hear him (7:16). They WILL go into captivity at this point. Even when God tells Judah through Jeremiah not to serve their other gods, they blatantly say, "we will certainly do whatsoever thing goeth forth out of our own mouth, to burn incense unto the queen of heaven, and to pour out drink offerings unto her" (44:17). The book of

Jeremiah shows the complete disregard that Judah has for God's Word, as the king of Judah throws God's holy words of judgment into the fire, as soon as they are read (36:22-25), showing no remorse for their wickedness. The result is that the book of Jeremiah ends with Judah going into captivity (52). The good news, though, is, because Judah is God's people, God will redeem them and judge Babylon in the end, when Judah finally turns to God (50). This redemption is accomplished by the Lord Jesus Christ (33:14-17). In the meantime, though, the book of **Lamentations** is written by Jeremiah to lament Judah going into Babylonian captivity. Even in the midst of this great lament, the believing remnant of Israel exclaims, "great is Thy faithfulness" (Lamentations 3:23).

Ezekiel is the major prophet writing to Judah during the Babylonian captivity (1:1-3). Judah must turn to God before the end of the 70 years of captivity in order to rebuild Jerusalem. Therefore, Ezekiel is called to do some crazy things to get Judah's attention. Ezekiel is to lie on his left side for 390 days for Israel's iniquity and then 40 days on his right side for Judah's iniquity (4:4-8). Even when they are taken captive, God promises to save a remnant that He will scatter among the nations (6:8-10). This is in fulfillment of the fifth cycle of chastisement, found in Leviticus 26, in which God promised to continue to punish Israel for their unbelief, so that they might believe, culminating in the fifth cycle in which He promises to scatter Israel "among the heathen" (Leviticus 26:33). Ezekiel 8-11 shows the glory of the Lord leaving the temple and eventually leaving Jerusalem altogether (11:22-23). Thus, because of their unbelief, Judah will go into captivity, and God has officially left the temple and Jerusalem. But, once Israel believes, at the end of the tribulation period, God will gather the believing remnant from the heathen and bring them back into the land of Israel (36:24).

To ensure that Israel never has to leave their land again, God makes a new covenant with them, putting His Spirit within them, causing them to obey His law covenant with them (36:25-28). This new covenant is not with us today and does not start in Matthew, as most Christians believe. It is with Israel, as Jeremiah 31:31 specifically says, "Behold, the days come, saith the Lord, that I will make a new covenant with the house of Israel, and with the house of Judah." Also, this new covenant does not begin until Jesus puts Israel in their land at His second coming. According to Ezekiel 37, this includes both Israel and Judah, re-united as one kingdom under the Lord Jesus Christ (37:18-22). Thus, present-day Mormons are not a part of this, as they love to twist this Ezekiel 37 passage to say that they are. Also, we see from 37:1-14, that the saved of Israel includes those faithful Jews, who have died before. Ezekiel 38 shows the final battle between God and Satan, which occurs after the millennial reign (Revelation 20:7-10). The remainder of Ezekiel is concerned with the temple, Israel in the land, and God and His throne in His eternal kingdom on earth.

The book of **Daniel** is written from Babylon during Judah's 70 years of Babylonian captivity. Daniel, Hananiah, Mishael, and Azariah are set aside as God's believing remnant, showing all of Babylon and, more importantly, all of Israel, that the Lord God of Israel is the Lord of all.

Daniel is probably the most important book for Israel to understand, from the time it is written until the time they enter God's kingdom. Daniel 1 shows them to trust in the Lord during the tribulation period, rather than eating food associated with the idolatry of the Antichrist. The result will be spiritual well being in the kingdom. Daniel 2 shows them that, until Jesus comes and establishes God's kingdom on earth, Israel will be ruled by Gentiles. Luke 21:24 refers to this time as "the times of the Gentiles." It is the Lord Jesus Christ as "the stone [that] was cut out of the mountain without hands" (Daniel 2:45), who sets up the kingdom for the God of heaven (Daniel 2:44). Daniel 3 shows that those, who trust in God's law covenant will be a part of that kingdom. Hananiah, Mishael, and Azariah are thrown into a fiery furnace, but the Lord is with them, such that the fiery furnace has no power over them, "nor was an hair of their head singed" (Daniel 3:27). Similarly, faithful Israel will go through the refiner's fire of the tribulation period (Malachi 3:2-4), and they will come out on the other side in God's kingdom without even losing a single hair (Matthew 10:30). Daniel 4 shows Nebuchadnezzar, the king of Babylon, being brought low (Daniel 4:33), just like God will destroy the Antichrist and his kingdom. Daniel 5 shows the Medes taking the kingdom away from Babylon, showing that Israel should not trust in man's kingdom, because it is temporary. Daniel 6 shows Daniel being thrown into a lion's den and not being killed, just like believing Israel will be in the tribulation period with "the devil, as a roaring lion, [walking] about, seeking whom he may devour" (I Peter 5:8), but the devil will not devour them.

Daniel 7-12 is a series of visions that Daniel receives. It reveals that the Antichrist will come at the end of the times of the Gentiles, and detail is given as to what he will do. Most of the visions are concentrated on the time of the Antichrist. The most significant vision is the 70 weeks found in Daniel 9:24-27. This is the most important passage for Israel to understand, because it tells them that 490 years remain in their history before the Lord Jesus Christ establishes God's kingdom on earth. It tells them that the Messiah will be cut off after 483 years, and that the last 7 years are marked by a covenant that the Antichrist makes with apostate Israel, which is the tribulation period. Once those 490 years are over, sin is done away with for Israel forever! Daniel ends with the commandment to "shut up the words, and seal the book" (12:4). Therefore, there are many end-time events revealed to Daniel that are not revealed to Israel as a whole until given in the book of Revelation.

Just like Isaiah's prophesying in the nude and Ezekiel's lying on his side for 430 days and using cow dung to prepare bread, God makes **Hosea** do a strange thing to get Israel's and Judah's attention (Hosea prophesied to both kingdoms in Israel.). God commands Hosea to marry a prostitute and have children by her (Hosea 1:2). He was to name his firstborn "Not my people" (Hosea 1:9). This was to be an illustration of God's relationship to Israel so that Israel may turn from their unbelief and have faith in God. Israel had played the whore against God by serving other gods, just like Hosea was to marry a prostitute. Therefore, God declares that Israel is "not My people," which is prophetic of the time from Acts 9 until the rapture, during which time God sets aside the nation of Israel and starts the body of Christ (more about that later). Yet, God does promise He will betroth Himself to Israel again (2:19-23) in the future, which is prophetic of the time after the rapture. Therefore, Hosea speaks of the coming judgment against Israel, which is the time of the Gentiles, but it does include a call to repentance (14:1-2), because God will save those in Israel, who trust in Him.

The book of **Joel** is written to Judah. The book looks at the current, spiritual depravity of Judah and issues a call to repentance. When they do turn to the Lord, He will bring about the events of the tribulation period so that He can purge the earth of the wicked nations and bring Judah into God's eternal kingdom on earth (Joel 2:28-3:21).

The book of **Amos** is prophecy written to both Israel and Judah. It is the bleakest of all the prophets, as it does nothing but talk about God pouring His wrath upon the world, with the exception of the last, five verses, which talk about God bringing Israel back into the land. Israel has turned so far away from God that He promises a period of time in which He will not speak to Israel (Amos 8:11-14). This "famine ... of hearing the words of the Lord" is the 400-year period between Malachi and Matthew.

The book of **Obadiah** is the shortest book in the Old Testament. He prophesies against Edom, which is the nation, started by Israel's brother, Esau. God curses

Edom for cursing Israel (v. 10), fulfilling God's promise to Abram in Genesis 12:3. Verses 17-21 show how God will give the spoils of Edom to Israel. Thus, Obadiah teaches Israel the lesson that, in spite of their wickedness and idolatry, God will restore them. Therefore, they should put their trust in God, which is the true context of Proverbs 3:5-6.

The book of **Jonah** is similar to Hosea, in that God gets him to do something crazy to get Israel's attention. God's special nation is Israel (Deuteronomy 7:6). There is no other nation to which God gave His law (Deuteronomy 4:7-8). Yet, God tells Jonah to go to Nineveh, the capital of Assyria, which was Israel's biggest enemy at the time, and tell them they will be destroyed. The implication is that, if Nineveh is sorry for their sins, God will forgive them and use them to destroy Israel. Therefore, God is basically saying, "Israel, you won't listen to Me. Okay. I'll save your enemy. Maybe that will show you that I am God, and you should have faith in Me, instead of your false gods." Therefore, Jonah's call is to save Israel's enemy and have them overthrow Israel. Knowing this, Jonah ran away (4:2). But, he eventually did what he was told (3:1-4), Nineveh believed God (3:5), and God saved them (3:10).

In Jonah, God pronounced judgment against Nineveh (Assyria's capital), they believed God, and God spared them. The book of **Micah** is written about God's judgment against both Samaria (Israel's capital) and Jerusalem (Judah's capital) (1:1). Will Israel follow the example of the Ninevites and believe God, so that He may spare them? Sadly, they will not. The first 3 chapters of Micah cover God's judgment against Israel and Judah. Then, the good news is given in Micah 4 that God will restore Israel in the last days and set up His kingdom in Mount Zion in Jerusalem (4:2). God does so through the Lord Jesus Christ, who will be born in Bethlehem, according to 5:2. Because God brings deliverance through the Christ, Israel and Judah are then called to turn from their religion and place their faith in God's deliverance instead (ch. 6).

Now, we mentioned that there were a few, good kings in Judah. Under those kings, idols were torn down, the house of the Lord was built up, and people began observing God's law again. Then, a bad king would rise up, and Judah would turn away from God and go into idolatry worse than before. Nineveh repented, under Jonah's preaching, and they were saved. However, they later turned from God. The book of **Nahum** is written to show that God will destroy Nineveh for turning back to idolatry. Thus, Nahum serves as an example to Judah that they are not okay, just because one generation served God. God will judge Judah for turning back away from God, just like He will judge Nineveh for turning back away from God after repenting under Jonah's preaching.

In spite of the wickedness and idolatry of Israel, as a whole, there is always a believing remnant, who have faith in God's law covenant with Israel. **Habakkuk** represents this believing remnant. Thus, Habakkuk is called a "burden" (1:1), rather than a prophecy. "How long shall I cry, and Thou wilt not hear!" (1:2), Habakkuk says. Babylon will come and bring Judah into captivity so that Judah, as a whole, may turn to God (1:6). This is the 70-year Babylonian captivity. Ultimately, it is the 7-year tribulation period, in which the Babylonian religious system will rule over Israel via the Antichrist, and that trial will cause all of the lost sheep of the house of Israel to turn to God and be saved. Apostate Israel will stay lost, but "the just shall live by his faith" (2:4). It is the trials of the 70-year Babylonian captivity in the short term and the 7-year tribulation period in the long term that will separate the wheat from the chaff (Matthew 13:29-30), such that all believing Israel shall be saved (Romans 11:26).

Habbakuk asked "O Lord, how long" (1:2), and the Lord answers in **Zephaniah**: Until the enemy in Judah is destroyed and the wicked nations are brought low. So imminent is God's judgment of Judah when Zephaniah is written that the first thing out of God's mouth is, "I will utterly consume all things from off the land" (1:2). Chapter 1 is all about that judgment. 2:1-3 tells Judah they can avoid God's wrath if they trust in God. Once that wrath is over, 2:4-15 speaks of God's judgment against the Gentiles. This frees up God, in chapter 3, to bring Israel into the land in His eternal kingdom on earth. It is "an afflicted and poor people" (3:12), i.e., the believing remnant, coming out of the tribulation period, that God will bring into His eternal kingdom on earth (3:13-20). It is a painful process for "the kingdom of God [to] be taken from [apostate Israel], and given to [the believing remnant], bringing forth the fruits thereof" (Matthew 21:43), and God must wait until the tribulation period to do so, because, only then, is Israel humbled enough to be saved.

Haggai speaks of the time when Israel will come back into the Promised Land. It tells the story of coming from Babylonian captivity to rebuild the temple. However, what is ultimately in God's mind is the building of the true temple of God, which is Israel, as we are told that "the glory of this latter house shall be greater than of the former" (2:9), referring to the temple in the kingdom, rather than the one that is built just after returning from Babylon.

The book of **Zechariah** is written just after the Babylonian captivity. Thus, God calls to Israel to "turn ye unto Me" (1:3). Again, God is ultimately looking to the tribulation period, in which Israel will return to Him. Jesus Christ will then dwell in Jerusalem in the kingdom forever (2:12). It is by His Spirit that He will gather Israel back to Himself (4:6). Zechariah shows God doing the work to reconcile Israel back to Himself. It is Israel's job just to have faith in what He is doing. It is Jesus, Who ultimately builds the temple (6:12-13), comes back to earth (14:4), destroys apostate Israel's religion (10:3), overthrows the Antichrist (11:17), brings Israel into the land (8:7-8), destroys the Gentiles, who are against the little flock of Israel (12:9), causes the remaining Gentiles to want to join themselves to God (8:22-23), and rules and reigns with Israel over the Gentiles in God's eternal kingdom on earth.

Malachi is the last prophet before the 400-year famine of hearing the word of the Lord (Amos 8:11). The first 3 chapters talk of how Israel has used religion to get away from God. In 3:1-4, God promises to refine Israel Himself, through the fire of the tribulation period so that they will be weaned off of their religion and will trust in God alone to bring them into the kingdom. Chapter 4 speaks of God reforming Israel by using Elijah to get Israel to go back to trusting in God's law covenant with Israel.

Around 400 BC, Judah is back in the land after their 70-year Babylonian captivity. There may have been a temporary turning back to God with the people who came back into the land, by their building the city and the temple in Jerusalem. However, they become more steeped in their religion, not heeding the warning of Malachi.

When God called Abram to start the nation of Israel, He said that Israel would wait 400 years in a strange land until the iniquity of those in the Promised Land became full (Genesis 15:13-16). Similarly, with apostate Israel in the Promised Land, God waits 400 years between Malachi and Matthew for their iniquity to become full so that He can prepare the way for the kingdom by making a "reconciliation for iniquity" (Daniel 9:24). If the Lord Jesus Christ does not wait 400 years, when He comes to establish the kingdom, He will, instead, have to "smite the earth with a curse" (Malachi 4:6).

New Testament

Once the 400 years pass, the kingdom of heaven is at hand (Matthew 3:2). This is where the book of Matthew begins. There are 2 things that must take place before

God can establish the kingdom. First, He must provide the sacrifice for sin (Isaiah 53:5-6). Second, Israel must be ready to be the priests of the Lord to the Gentiles, so that they may be saved, as well (Isaiah 61:6).

The books of Matthew through John show the Lord Jesus Christ Himself, fulfilling the 4 aspects of the Christ that were prophesied in the Old Testament. Matthew shows Him as Israel's king (Jeremiah 23:5), who will bind Satan, take him off the throne, and sit on the throne Himself (Matthew 12:28-29). Mark shows Him as Israel's servant (Isaiah 42:1), Who would provide the sacrifice for Israel's sins, so that they can enter the kingdom. Luke shows Him as Israel's man (Zechariah 6:12), Who lives a perfect, sinless life, so that His sacrifice for their sins will meet the justice of God, while appeasing His wrath against sin. John shows Him as Israel's God (Isaiah 40:9), Who has the power to take them from being in Satan's grasp (Jeremiah 31:11) and bring them into the kingdom.

The next step in the process is to prepare Israel to have faith in God to bring them into the kingdom. All 3 members of the Godhead are needed for this. God the Father sends John the Baptist (John 1:6) to prepare the way for the Lord (Matthew 3:3). Unfortunately, Israel beheads him (Matthew 14:10). God the Son comes to Israel in the person of the Lord Jesus Christ. Unfortunately, Israel crucifies Him (Matthew 27:25). In spite of the warning that the Holy Ghost is the only member of the Godhead left for them to reject (Matthew 12:31-32), Israel rejects Him in Acts 2-7 with their final rejection of Him being the stoning of Stephen (The one-year ministry of the Holy Ghost during Acts 2-7 is prophesied by Jesus Christ in Luke 13:6-9.). Thus, God accomplishes His purpose in Matthew – John, but Israel fails to believe (John 12:37).

The book of **Matthew** shows Jesus as Israel's king. He says, in Matthew 15:24, that He is "not sent but unto the lost sheep of the house of Israel." Thus, He is Israel's king. Matthew 1 connects His genealogy to King David (1:1). He is treated as a king by the three wise men (2). The way is prepared for the king by John the Baptist (3). Jesus frees people, bound by Satan's kingdom (4:23-25). He gives His people His law (5-7). When Israel rejects Him as king (12:24-27), He stops giving clear instructions to Israel and speaks to them in parables so that they may not understand the mysteries of the kingdom (13:10-11), since they are outsiders. He prepares the believing remnant to take over for Him, by appointing Peter the leader while Christ is not on the earth, giving Peter the authority to forgive or not forgive sins (16:18-19). Jesus shows His people His coming glory in the kingdom (17:1-5). In the meantime, He shows His disciples that He has not been accepted as Israel's king yet (21:1-11), but the believing remnant will accept Him as king (21:43). He warns the believing remnant of the false kingdom, which is apostate Israel (23). He tells them how they will know this false kingdom is coming to an end (24). He tells them of the Jews (25:1-30) and the Gentiles (25:31-46), who will be part of His kingdom. We see the false kingdom's plot to overthrow Christ as king (26-27) by crucifying Him. Jesus' resurrection shows that plot is not successful, and Christ sends His disciples out to build up His kingdom (28), since, as the conquering king, "all power is given unto [Jesus] in heaven and in earth" (28:18).

The book of **Mark** shows Jesus as the servant. As such, no genealogy is given. A servant works. Therefore, 12 of Mark's 16 chapters begin with the word "and." Jesus works and never stops in Mark. By the time we get to Mark 1:14, Jesus has already been baptized, tempted for 40 days, and has started working in His earthly ministry. He picks disciples (1:16-20), and starts casting out the enemy (1:23-26,34). The instructions Jesus gives healed people in Mark often include, "see thou say nothing to any man" (1:44), because a servant is not supposed to be recognized for his work (Luke 17:10). The Sermon on the Mount (Matthew 5-7) is not included, because a servant is not in a position of authority. Mark shows Jesus performing the signs of the kingdom, using parables, being crucified, and rising from the dead. When Jesus commissions His disciples, He tells them to work (Mark 16:15-20). Thus, the signs of the kingdom are appropriate here, and should not be excluded as modern versions like to do.

The book of **Luke** shows Jesus as the perfect man. It covers much of the same information as Matthew does but with more detail at times. Luke is the only one to give detail surrounding John the Baptist's birth (1) and to go into detail on the believing remnant's reaction to Jesus' birth (2:25-38). Since Luke shows Jesus as a man, His genealogy goes all the way back to God and Adam (3:23-38). The good Samaritan (10:30-37), the lost sheep (15:1-7), the lost coin (15:8-10), the lost son (15:11-32), the rich man and Lazarus (16:19-31), the persistent widow (18:1-8), the Pharisee and the publican (18:9-14), and Zacchaeus (19:1-10) are stories only found in Luke, because they are examples of how the men of Israel should respond to the perfect man, Jesus. Jesus sets His Own example of the perfect man by praying so earnestly that, with regard to the cross, He only overcomes the flesh by sweating "as it were great drops of blood" (22:44). Only Luke records this detail. Luke is also the only one to record Jesus speaking to the two men on the road to Emmaus (24:13-32), as it shows how a believing man in Israel is to share scripture with the lost sheep of the house of Israel (24:27, 44-46), so that they may believe, too. Finally, it is the only gospel to share Jesus' ascension (24:51), as a sign of how believing Israel will not perish with this world at Jesus' second coming.

Matthew – Luke are called "the synoptic gospels," meaning that they share similar information. While there are similarities, we have seen that each gospel shows a different aspect of the Christ. Rather than seeing Matthew – Luke as similar, we should see **John** as very different. John is different, because it shows Jesus as God. It is a great understatement to say there are great differences between what man and what God does. Thus, a great contrast is seen between Matthew – Luke and John, when all four show a different aspect of the Messiah.

Since John shows Jesus as God, the genealogy is of His deity (1:1-2). We also see John the Baptist in the light of being sent by God (1:6). The first miracle John shares is turning water into wine (2:1-11), because it shows what God is doing for Israel by saving them and bringing them into the kingdom. Thus, only John records this miracle. The religious leaders are usually called by their name (Pharisees, priests, scribes, Sadducees, etc.) in Matthew – Luke, but John, taking God's perspective, refers to them as "the Jews"—as this term appears 64 times in John and only 16 times in Matthew – Luke combined. Nicodemus is used in John alone, as an example of a religious leader who: 1) Questions his religion (3:1-2), 2) Speaks against his religion (7:50-51), and 3) Becomes a member of the believing remnant (19:38-40). This shows that Jesus, as God, can convert anyone, including the religious folks. He can also convert the Samaritans, even though they were hated by the Jews in Jerusalem. The woman at the well shows Samaria going from being "not My people" to being "the sons of the living God" (Hosea 1:10). This is what John 4 is all about. John 5 tells of the man at Bethesda being healed. This story is only found in John, because he was sick for 38 years (5:5), which is the time that Israel was spiritually sick in the wilderness (Deuteronomy 2:14), showing that Jesus, as God, can also heal evil unbelievers.

Romans 10:17 says, "faith cometh by hearing, and hearing by the word of God." Since John shows Jesus as God and He is "the Word" (John 1:1), most of the book of John reveals Jesus as Israel's God, since "salvation is of the Jews" (4:22). In the Old Testament, God revealed Himself to Israel as the "I AM" (Exodus 3:14). Jesus never calls Himself the "I AM" in Matthew – Luke, but He does call Himself "I AM" 14 times in John (6:35, 6:41, 6:48, 6:51, 8:12, 8:58, 10:7, 10:9, 10:11, 10:14, 11:25, 14:6, 15:1, and 15:5).

In John 8, Jesus shows "the Jews" that they are not Abraham's seed, because they do not believe God's Word (8:33-40). Instead, they are children of the devil (8:44). Jesus shows them this so that they may come to Him, the "living bread" (6:51), and have faith in God's Word, rather than in the Jewish religion. Unfortunately, in the healing of the blind man, in John 9, we see the Jews continue to hold to their religion and reject God's Word.

John 11-19 all occur in the one-week period before Jesus' crucifixion. Jesus shows He is God by raising Lazarus from the dead (11:43-44), which foreshadows Jesus raising Himself from the dead. Note the power that Jesus displays with regard to His death and resurrection. He says, "I lay down my life....No man taketh it from me....I have power to lay it down, and I have power to take it again" (10:17-18). Only God could make such a statement! When Judas is about to betray Jesus, it is Jesus who orders him to go ahead: "That thou doest, do quickly" (13:27). There is no agonizing prayer in the garden before His death in John, because Jesus, as God, does not agonize over the cross. Instead, chapters 14-16 show Him giving instructions to His disciples with chapter 17 being the true Lord's prayer for the believing remnant of Israel. When the soldiers come to arrest Jesus, Jesus says, "I am he," which causes the band of arresting men to go backward and fall to the ground (18:6). Only God's Word could have such an effect on men. John concludes with Jesus, after His resurrection, commanding Peter to take care of the little flock for Him (21:15-17). Thus, everything Jesus does in John shows that He is God, which is why the book of John is so much different from Matthew – Luke.

A significant change occurs

The book of **Acts** shows Israel's history after the cross. The Holy Ghost is given in Acts 2. The nation, as a whole, rejects God's law covenant with them for the final time, as they reject the ministry of the Holy Ghost. Jesus had said, "Whosoever speaketh against the Holy Ghost, it shall not be forgiven him" (Matthew 12:32). Thus, when Israel makes their final rejection of the Holy Ghost with the stoning of Stephen, Jesus STANDS at the right hand of God (Acts 7:55-56).

Old Testament scripture shows that Jesus' standing at the right hand of God is incredibly significant. Psalm 110:1 says that God the Father instructed God the Son to "SIT Thou at My right hand, until I make Thine enemies Thy footstool." Acts 2:23 says, in talking to Israel, "Ye have taken, and by wicked hands have crucified and slain" Jesus. Therefore, "Thine enemies," according to Acts 2:23, are Israel. Isaiah 3:13-14 says, "The Lord standeth up to plead, and standeth to judge the people. The Lord will enter into judgment with the ancients of His people, and the princes thereof: for ye have eaten up the vineyard; the spoil of the poor is in your houses." The vineyard is the house of Israel, according to Isaiah 5:7. Thus, Jesus' STANDING at the right hand of God, in Acts 7:55-56, says that God has judged Israel as apostate and is now setting aside His plan to reconcile the earth back to Himself through the nation of Israel. He does not end this plan, because "the gifts and calling of God are without repentance" (Romans 11:29). Therefore, God will still reconcile the earth back to Himself through the nation of Israel. However, He sets this plan aside for now, because the kingdom of heaven is at hand, and Israel is not ready to enter it, even though they are supposed to be God's kingdom of priests in the kingdom to reach the Gentiles with the gospel.

In Genesis 1:1, God created the heaven and the earth. The next verse starts with, "and the earth." From Genesis 1:2 through Acts 7:60, God's focus has been on the earth. Beginning with Acts 9, God shifts His focus to the heaven. "The heavens are not clean in His sight" (Job 15:15), because Satan (Ezekiel 28:15-16) and 1/3 of the angels rebelled against God (Revelation 12:4). Therefore, the heaven needs to be reconciled back to God, just like the earth. However, if God had talked about His plan to reconcile the heaven back to Himself before, Satan "would not have crucified the Lord of glory" (I Corinthians 2:8).

In order to reconcile both the earth and the heaven back to God, Jesus had to die on a cross. The Old Testament never mentions this. The Old Testament says that the Christ would die for the sins of Israel (Isaiah 53:3-8), and He would do so by being sacrificed on the altar in the temple in Jerusalem (Psalm 118:27), as the ultimate Passover Lamb to take away their sins (John 1:29). Therefore, when Jesus came into Jerusalem, Satan got the Jewish leaders to arrest Him and send Him off to the Romans to keep Him from being sacrificed on the altar as the atonement for Israel's sins. What Satan did not know is that, by being "lifted up" on the cross, He would "draw ALL men" to Himself (John 12:32). In other words, both Jews and Gentiles were involved in His crucifixion, which gives both Jews and Gentiles the opportunity to be saved. Therefore, Jesus did not "give his life a ransom for many" on the altar (Matthew 20:28), but He gave His life "a ransom for all, to be testified in due time" (I Timothy 2:6) on the cross. Paul was an apostle "born out of due time" (I Corinthians 15:7-8) to give this testimony.

Therefore, once Israel is set aside, God calls Paul in Acts 9 to go to the whole world, and not just to the Jews. The Lord said about Paul that, "he is a chosen vessel unto Me, to bear My name before the Gentiles, and kings, and the children of Israel" (Acts 9:15). Not only that, but Paul was given new information to preach. What Peter preached to Israel in early Acts was what "God hath spoken by the mouth of all His holy prophets since the world began" (Acts 3:21). What Paul preached, beginning in Acts 9, was "the mystery, which was kept secret since the world began, But now is made manifest" (Romans 16:25-26). This new information was that salvation comes by trusting in Jesus' death, burial, and resurrection, as atonement for sins (I Corinthians 15:3-4), rather than repenting and being baptized for the remission of sins, as Peter said (Acts 2:38).

Paul said, "a dispensation of the gospel is committed unto me" (I Corinthians 9:17). It was in Paul "FIRST" that "Jesus Christ might shew forth all longsuffering, for a pattern to them which should hereafter believe on Him to life everlasting" (I Timothy 1:16). Paul said, "the gospel which was preached of me is not after man. For I neither received it of man, neither was I taught it, but by the revelation of Jesus Christ" (Galatians 1:11-12). He preached "the dispensation of God which is given to me for you, to fulfill the word of God" (Colossians 1:25).

When God called Paul, He had set aside Israel's program. However, God still wanted Israel to be saved. Therefore, God gave Israel the opportunity to be saved under this new program committed to Paul. It is Paul's going to Israel that is shown from Acts 9 through the end of Acts. In this portion of Acts, we see Paul preaching "the gospel ... to the Jew first, and also to the Greek" (Romans 1:16). Thus, Paul's pattern is to go to the Jewish synagogue, preach the gospel, and then go to the Gentiles with the gospel.

Just like we saw Israel reject the gospel of the kingdom 3 times in Acts 1-7 (see Acts 4:15-18; 5:17-18; 7:54-59), we see Israel reject the gospel of the grace of God 3 times in Acts 13:44-46, 18:5-6, and 28:25-28. This period of time is called "the diminishing of" Israel (Romans 11:12). Israel diminished away, and Paul focused exclusively on the Gentiles after Acts 28, as "the apostle of the Gentiles" (Romans 11:13). That is why the book of Acts ends after chapter 28. It has shown the fall of Israel in rejecting the gospel of the kingdom, preached by Peter and the believing remnant of Israel, and it has shown the diminishing away of Israel in rejecting the gospel of the grace of God under Paul's ministry. Thus, Acts ends, not with Paul's death, but with Israel's death, having rejected God's salvation, both in earthly places and in heavenly places.

Since Paul was given new information, He needed to write it down for us today, and that information is found in Romans – Philemon. Therefore, while Genesis – Acts was written to Israel in time past, Romans – Philemon is written to the church, the body of Christ today. "All scripture is given by inspiration of God, and is profitable for doctrine, for reproof, for correction for instruction in righteousness" (II Timothy 3:16). All scripture is FOR you, but only Romans – Philemon is written TO you today.

Most Christians take great offense to the statement that we should not follow the instructions given by Jesus Christ in Matthew – John. However, those taking this stance do not try to follow all instructions contained in the Bible. For example, they do not believe the gospel is to trust that God will make their seed like the stars of heaven, as it was to Abraham (Genesis 15:5-6), and they do not believe that it is a sin to wear a shirt with mixed fibers in it, even though God specifically prohibits this practice in Leviticus 19:19. They recognize that the Old Testament law is not for them to follow today, because it was not given to them. They need to recognize the same for Matthew – John. Jesus was sent by the Father only "unto the lost sheep of the house of Israel" (Matthew 15:24). "Jesus Christ was a minister of the circumcision for the truth of God, to confirm the promises made unto the fathers" (Romans 15:8), i.e., Abraham, Isaac, and Jacob. Jesus said that "salvation is of the Jews" (John 4:22), while Paul says that, today, "there is no respect of persons with God" (Romans 2:11).

They also do not follow what Jesus said. For example, they do not sell all their worldly possessions, as Jesus commanded all of His followers to do (Luke 12:33). They also do not observe the Mosaic law, even though that is what Jesus said to do (Matthew 23:2-3). How many Christians circumcise their male children, as Jesus was circumcised, go through the days of purification after giving birth to a child, as Mary did, or provide a sacrifice for the firstborn son, all according to the Mosaic law (Luke 2:21-24)?

The reason given for elevating what Jesus said over what Paul said is that Jesus was God, while Paul was just a man. While that is true, Jesus came as a man, and spoke and did only what God the Father told Him to speak and do (John 12:49-50; 14:10; 5:19,30). Romans – Philemon is just as much a part of God's Word as Matthew – John is. I Corinthians 14:37 tells us that Paul's epistles "are the commandments of the Lord." Since those commandments are to us today, they are the ones we should follow, rather than the commandments of the Lord given to the Jews by Jesus in Matthew – John.

It is vitally important that we make this distinction and follow God's Word to us today through Paul's epistles, and not God's Word to the Jews in time past in Matthew – John, because both cannot be followed at the same time. For example, the Lord said through Jesus that "if ye forgive men their trespasses, your heavenly Father will also forgive you: But if ye forgive not men their trespasses, neither will your Father forgive your trespasses" (Matthew 6:14-15). And, the Lord said through Paul, "Be ye kind one to another, tenderhearted, forgiving one another, even as God for Christ's sake hath forgiven you" (Ephesians 4:32). Both are God's commandments and both are true, but it is impossible for both to be true at the same time. The same holds for working. The Lord said through Jesus, "Take no thought for your life, what ye shall eat, or what ye shall drink; nor yet for your body, what ye shall put on …. Behold the fowls of the air: for they sow not, neither do they reap, nor gather into barns; yet your heavenly Father feedeth them. Are ye not much better than they?" (Matthew 6:25-26). And, the Lord said through Paul, "But if any provide not for his own, and specially for those of his own house, he hath denied the faith, and is worse than an infidel" (I Timothy 5:8). Again, both are God's commandments and both are true, but they cannot both be followed at the same time.

Thus, having recognized that we should only follow the commandments the Lord gives us in Paul's epistles (Romans – Philemon), let us look at what these books tell us. Scripture is given "for doctrine, for reproof, for correction, for instruction in righteousness" (II Timothy 3:16). Paul's epistles follow this pattern. Romans gives doctrine, I & II Corinthians reproves a lack of practical application of Romans doctrine, and Galatians corrects false doctrine related to the doctrine given in Romans. This same pattern is followed in Ephesians – Colossians with more advanced doctrine for those who have already learned and are practically living out Romans doctrine. I & II Thessalonians gives more doctrine. Then, I & II Timothy and Titus give "instruction in righteousness" for how the church is to operate. Philemon puts it all together with an example of a man, whose life is transformed, as a result of learning the doctrine found in Paul's epistles.

Now, let us look at Paul's epistles in more detail. **Romans** gives doctrine of what the cross of Christ means to people today. Romans 1:1 – 3:20 shows that all people are worthy of eternal damnation in the lake of fire. Romans 3:21 – 5:21 shows that Jesus Christ's death, burial, and resurrection atone for the sins of all of those who believe in it, and that, upon believing, a person has "NOW [been] justified by His blood" and has "NOW received the atonement" (Romans 5:9,11). Romans 6 – 8, then, teaches that we have been baptized into Jesus' death and raised with Him into eternal life. Thus, we have the ability to allow the Holy Spirit to live through us so that we serve God, rather than serving our own flesh. Romans 9 – 11 addresses what happened to Israel's program and brings both Israel's program and today's programs full circle, showing that, once "the fulness of the Gentiles be come in" (Romans 11:25), i.e., once the rapture takes place, Israel's program will pick back up, such that "all Israel shall be saved" (Romans 11:26).

Romans 12:4-5 teaches that all people saved today are part of the body of Christ. Romans 12 – 16 shows how the practical application of Romans 1 – 8 doctrine is lived out, such that, if a local group of believers follow it, God will bruise Satan under their feet (Romans 16:20).

The book of **I Corinthians** is written to a bunch of carnal Christians (I Corinthians 3:1-3), who are carnal because they do not believe Romans doctrine. Thus, the Lord addresses their carnality in this book. Chapter 1 says that God's wisdom is foolish to man. Chapter 2 says that, what Paul is saying, was kept secret until revealed to Him, and that the doctrine for today is revealed to members of the body of Christ today, as they allow the Holy Spirit to teach it to them as they read God's Word. Chapter 3 covers the carnality of the Corinthians, and teaches them that they will only be rewarded for allowing the Holy Spirit to work through them. Chapter 4 shows that serving the Lord will subject the Corinthians to persecution by the world.

The rest of I Corinthians covers specific issues the Corinthians are having because they do not have sound, Romans doctrine built into their souls. Chapter 5 covers fornication. Chapter 6 covers sins done against each other, and how they are to separate themselves from believers not walking in the Spirit. Chapter 7 covers how a saint should view marriage. Chapter 8 teaches them not to offend those weaker in sound doctrine, so that they can grow up in the doctrine over time. Chapter 9 is Paul's example to them of catering to the weak so that others may be saved and edified in the doctrine. Chapter 10 shows the bad, spiritual example of Israel and how to act around religious folks. Chapters 11-14 deals with godly conduct within church services, showing that charity (chapter 13) and the edification of others (chapter 14) are to be made a priority. Chapter 15 gives proper doctrine regarding resurrection. Chapter 16 covers proper conduct to other local assemblies of the body of Christ.

I Corinthians corrected a failure by the Corinthians to have the practical application of Romans 6-8 doctrine demonstrated in their lives. Since "all that will live godly in Christ Jesus shall suffer persecution" (II Timothy 3:12), if the Corinthians apply I Corinthians and live godly, they need the doctrine of **II Corinthians** to help them not to abandon sound doctrine when they suffer. Thus, chapter 1 of II Corinthians talks about the comfort that God provides for those suffering for serving Christ. Chapter 2 warns of the danger of being legalistic to those who have sinned and come back to the fellowship, having turned from the sin. Chapter 3 talks about how the grace, that we enjoy in the body of Christ, is much better than the law that Israel was under. This is important to understand because the danger is to become legalistic, thinking there is power in that. Chapter 4 shows how suffering in the flesh is how God draws people to Himself. Thus, the suffering should be welcomed. Chapter 5 gets their focus on the spiritual by showing that we are new creatures in Christ. Thus, if the Corinthians suffer, or are even killed, for walking in the Spirit, they should not be concerned over it. Chapter 6 says that the suffering is what separates believers from those who practice church, so that the Corinthians may fulfill their ministry of reconciling others to God. Chapter 7 goes over the mental anguish that can take place when you walk in the Spirit and shows that God will comfort you, if you remain in the sound doctrine found in Paul's epistles. Chapters 8-9 shows that liberal, monetary giving leads to liberal, spiritual growth, because it takes the focus off the flesh, when it comes to money, so that money can be used to grow spiritually, rather than as the root of all evil (I Timothy 6:10). Because sound doctrine is so contrary to the flesh, what Paul has shared is the opposite of what their "ten thousand instructors in Christ" (I Corinthians 4:15) have shared with them. Therefore, Paul spends the rest of the book (chapters 10-13) defending himself as their apostle. He gives details of his suffering so that they see that suffering is, in fact, a proof of godly living. This will keep them from following false instructors and apostles, and it will comfort them in times of their own suffering for godly living.

The book of **Galatians** is all about showing that legalism is serving your own flesh. Walking in the Spirit means standing in the liberty we have in Christ. In the first 2 chapters, Paul has to defend himself to show he is preaching God's Word for today, and that his message is different from what the elders of the believing remnant from Israel's program are teaching. Back in Genesis 15, I made the point that the covenant God made with Abraham there was with him as a Gentile. In Galatians 3, Paul brings up that covenant to show that that covenant is what makes it possible to be justified by faith alone, and the true meaning of that covenant was kept a secret until revealed to Paul by the Holy Ghost here. Chapter 4 tells us that this covenant establishes us as heirs of God, because we have been adopted as His adult sons. This redeems us from the law system and puts us under grace. Thus, we should cast out the bondwoman of the law, because we have been made children of the free woman. Chapter 5 gives a contrast between the works of the flesh and walking in the Spirit. As Christians, we should put to death those works of the flesh. Paul concludes Galatians with chapter 6, showing that those, who have put to death the lusts of the flesh, can now help others in the church to do the same thing.

Romans gives fundamental doctrine regarding what the cross of Christ means to us today. **Ephesians** builds upon this foundation by telling us what we have been given in heavenly places, as a result of the cross of Christ, so that we may live, according to who we are in Christ. Chapter 1 talks about our blessings in Christ, shows that Christ is above all powers, and will use the body of Christ to fill all of the heavenly positions, which Satan and his devils lost due to their rebellion against God. Chapter 2 talks about us already being seated in heavenly places in Christ, as part of the holy temple that God is building with us, as we walk in the good works that God will do through us when we yield our bodies over to God as instruments of righteousness. Chapter 3 reminds the Ephesians that the only way they can walk in the Spirit is by learning the doctrine found in Paul's epistles, since all of the instructions, regarding heavenly places, were kept a secret from man until revealed to Paul. Chapter 4 shows Christ's power over all, as He started the body of Christ with spiritual gifts and is finishing it with His completed word to us today. Walking in this sound doctrine is what will show the world the love of Christ. Chapter 5 shows how learning and walking in the sound doctrine is what life is all about for those seated in heavenly places in Christ. Just like Christ died so that He could create a holy church, we ought to yield our flesh to God so that He can create a holy temple in us. Chapter 6 shows that everything we do has spiritual implications, and that our war is a spiritual one. Therefore, we need to use the spiritual weapon of God's Word with prayer in all situations in order to live as saints in an ungodly world.

The book of **Philippians** deals with correcting practical application from not understanding the doctrine of heavenly places and lifestyles found in Ephesians. Chapter 1 shows that thinking like Christ, by using God's Word and prayer, will result in the fruits of righteousness being displayed. Such a focus on the spiritual will cause you to value the spiritual over the flesh, even to the point of not being concerned about living or dying. Chapter 2 gives 2 examples of this. The first example is Jesus Christ, who did just that in coming to earth as a man, living a perfect life, and then having his life cut short by being crucified on a cross. Epaphroditus is the second example. He almost died "for the work of Christ" (2:30), because he recognized that walking in the Spirit is much more important than even physical breathing. In chapter 3, Paul gives his own example of giving up the wealth and power that he had in religion, counting those things as dung, so that he might know Christ, ending with the exhortation for the Philippians to "be thus minded" (3:15) and to "be followers together of me" (3:17), recognizing that we are already seated with Christ in heavenly places (3:20-21). Chapter 4 says that, if you have this mind, you will be content, regardless of the circumstance, and your thoughts will only be good. This may seem impossible in bad circumstances, but "I can do all things through Christ which strengtheneth me" (4:13), as "God shall supply all your need" (4:19) in having God's attitude toward life.

The book of **Colossians** corrects false doctrine, regarding who we are in Christ, i.e., the heavenly places we are seated in, the heavenly lifestyle we should live, and the heavenly attitude that we should have. As such, Colossians 1 is a lot like Ephesians 1. Paul focuses on the hope we have in heaven (v. 5), walking worthy of this hope (v. 10), and Christ being above all powers and putting us in positions of authority in heavenly places in Him (vs. 16-18). Chapter 2 focuses on who we are in Christ. We are complete in Him (v. 10), we have been spiritually circumcised (v. 11), we have been spiritually baptized into His death, and we have been raised from the dead with Him (v. 12). Therefore, rather than following the law (vs. 14-16) and religion (vs. 20-21), we should be following the Head's, i.e. Christ's, doctrine, which is only found today in Paul's epistles (v. 19). Chapter 3 says that, if we are following the Head, we will set our affections on things above (v. 2), put to death the deeds of the flesh (vs. 5-9), and put on the new man of Christ (vs. 10-17). 3:18 – 4:6 gives practical application of how the doctrine should work in your relationships with others. Then, 4:7-18 lists people who are walking in the doctrine, as examples for the Colossians.

I & II Thessalonians are the last books of doctrine for this dispensation. They say that our hope is in the resurrection life to come, rather than in this life on earth. The Thessalonians are already sound in Romans and Ephesians doctrine. If they have faith in their coming resurrection, they will "walk worthy of God" (I Thessalonians 2:12) and "walk and ... please God" (I Thessalonians 4:1). I Thessalonians 4 is all about this walk being based on the rapture, which is mentioned in 4:13-18. I Thessalonians 5, then, gives them practical application. If they have faith (Romans), charity (Ephesians), and hope (Thessalonians) working in them, they will always rejoice, always pray, always give thanks, always walk in the Spirit, and always make the right decisions (I Thessalonians 5:16-22), showing the world that God has wholly sanctified them for His service (I Thessalonians 5:23).

In II Thessalonians, we see that they have faith and charity (1:3) and endure persecutions (1:4). However, they will not continue to endure for long if they continue to believe that the wicked will not be punished for persecuting them (1:7). Chapter 2, then, covers the second coming of Christ and the events leading up to it, so that the Thessalonians will continue to endure persecutions for Christ. Chapter 3 is a warning to remove themselves from those who do not work and are gossips, because these people will keep the Thessalonians from serving Christ.

I Timothy, II Timothy, and Titus are written to Timothy and Titus, who Paul had appointed as leaders of churches in Ephesus and Crete, respectively. Now that Paul has already covered all the sound doctrine that we need to know today, he now covers proper church order and operations.

I Timothy 1 warns against false teachers and tells Timothy to listen to the sound doctrine of the Lord Jesus Christ as given to Paul, while kicking out those, who try to teach false doctrine and refuse to receive correction. I Timothy 2 talks about men and women operating properly in the church so that others may be saved and come unto the knowledge of the truth (v. 4). Chapter 3 goes over the qualifications of the bishop (who we call "pastor" today) and deacons. Chapter 4 warns that, as time goes on, more people will follow false doctrine. Therefore, Paul gives Timothy the exhortation to keep preaching sound doctrine, regardless of how small his congregation may become, as a result. Chapter 5 talks about how elders and widows should be treated by the church. Chapter 6 warns that most people follow after money. Therefore, most churches are going to forsake sound doctrine in favor of false doctrine that will bring more money into the church leaders' pockets. Timothy is exhorted to "keep that [sound doctrine] which is committed to [his] trust" (6:20).

Paul says in **II Timothy** 1 that "all they which are in Asia be turned away from me" (1:15). Therefore, he sees the crowds dwindle, leaving sound doctrine for the things of this world. Regardless of what people do, Timothy should "hold fast the form of sound words" (1:13). II Timothy 2 is another exhortation to sound doctrine by "rightly dividing the word of truth" (v. 15), which means recognizing the Bible's different instructions for the different time periods. Staying true to the doctrine enables Timothy to teach other men to be bishops (v. 2) and to correct those who are into false doctrine (vs. 23-26). Chapter 3 warns that most people follow religion, rather than sound doctrine. It ends with the reminder that following scripture, rather than "Christianity," will make you complete in Christ (vs. 16-17). Chapter 4 warns that the time will come when people will not even "endure" (v. 3) sound doctrine, much less believe it. Paul even mentions some former church leaders, who have gone astray. However, if Timothy fights the good fight of faith (v. 7), the Lord will preserve him in Christ (v. 18).

Titus chapters 1 and 3 warn Titus of the false teachers, who will come into the church, and how to deal with them so that they do not lead people astray. Chapter 2 goes over godly living, specifically for old men, old women, young women, young men, and servants.

Philemon shows how the sound doctrine of the Lord Jesus Christ found in Paul's epistles can completely transform a person from being lost and bound for hell to being a saint of God and profitable for the ministry.

Another significant change occurs

Romans 11:25-26 says: "Blindness in part is happened to Israel, until the fulness of the Gentiles be come in. And so all Israel shall be saved." Once the Lord Jesus Christ has enough members of the body of Christ to fill all the positions in heavenly places that the devil and his angels will be kicked out of, the fulness of the Gentiles are come in. At that time, all members of the body of Christ are raptured up into heaven, and the heavenly places are reconciled back to God (I Thessalonians 4:16-17; Revelation 12:7-9).

God, then, shifts His focus back to reconciling the earth back to Himself through the nation of Israel. God picks up in the plan right where He left off in Acts 7 with Israel in apostasy. The Antichrist comes as "the Christ" and establishes a seven-year covenant with Israel (Daniel 9:26-27), known as the tribulation period. After that, there is Jesus' second coming, when God sets up His eternal kingdom on earth with Israel ruling with Him over the Gentiles (Psalm 2:8, Revelation 2:26-27).

Israel goes from being apostate to being saved during those seven years. Hosea 1:10 says, "where it was said unto them, Ye are not my people, there it shall be said unto them, Ye are the sons of the living God." Malachi 3:2-4 says that this is the time of God's refining fire, when He purifies Israel to make them a pleasant offering unto the Lord. Revelation 11:3-7 says that God sends His two witnesses for the first half of the tribulation period, and those two witnesses end up getting at least 144,000 Jews saved before they are done (Revelation 7:3-8). However, Israel must "endure unto the end" of the tribulation period in order to be saved (Matthew 24:13). Since "without faith it is impossible to please" God (Hebrews 11:6) and "faith cometh by hearing ... the Word of God" (Romans 10:17), God gives them scripture specifically for this time period.

This scripture is Hebrews – Revelation, which is the last section of the Bible.

Thus, Hebrews – Revelation saves Israel during the tribulation period, like Romans – Philemon saves man from Paul's call in Acts 9 until the still-future rapture of the body of Christ.

The book of **Hebrews** gives doctrine of what the cross means to Israel in the tribulation period, much like Romans gives doctrine of what the cross means to the body of Christ today. Although most Christians today try to apply Hebrews to themselves, it should be obvious that the book of "Hebrews" is written to the Hebrews.

Hebrews chapters 1-2 show how Jesus Christ was set apart by God the Father to be the sacrifice for the sins of Israel. Chapters 3-4 show Him as being greater than Moses and warns them that, like Israel in the wilderness, the offer to enter the Promised Land is only available "To day" (3:7). Once "To day" is gone, which to them is Jesus' second coming, they cannot enter the Promised Land. Therefore, they had better have faith "To day" for God to redeem them through His law covenant (for Jesus is greater than Moses), just like the thief on the cross did (Luke 23:40-43). Chapters 5-6 show Jesus as being greater than the Levitical priests, which is why He can redeem believing Israel. He is a Melchisedecean priest, and chapter 7 shows why a Melchisedecean priest is better than a Leviitical priest, which means He brings a better covenant than the Levites did (7:22), which chapter 8 expounds upon. Chapters 9-10 show Jesus bringing a better sacrifice than the Levites did ("the offering of the body of Jesus Christ once for all" (10:10)), and that He is perfect. Therefore, He can enter the holy of holies in heaven to bring that sacrifice to God, so as to bring in the new covenant. The down side of this is that this gives Israel a greater accountability, which explains the warning in 10:26-39. The focus has now shifted from what Jesus did to what Israel must do to enter into that covenant. Encouragement is given to them in chapter 11, showing them the great people of faith before them. This culminates in the faith example of Jesus in 12:2-3. Chapters 12-13, then, have the Hebrews look unto Jesus as their example so that, even though they may have to endure trials during the tribulation period after they have believed God's law covenant with them, they will go forth unto Him and bear His reproach (13:12-13).

Like Hebrews, **James** is written to Israel for the tribulation period, as they are scattered among the heathen (1:1), according to the fifth and final cycle of chastisement in Leviticus 26:33. They are living in a time when the religion of the Antichrist will replace the commandments of God (Mark 7:8-9), such that faith in God will go by the wayside. Therefore, James 1-2 concentrate on having faith and keeping faith in God's provision, rather than trusting in the Babylonian religion of the Antichrist during the tribulation period. They also need to endure unto the end of the tribulation period in order to be saved (Matthew 10:22). Therefore, they are justified by faith plus works (James 2:24), instead of faith alone, like today (Romans 3:28). Chapter 3 shows how powerful words are. The practical application of this is in chapter 4 that they need to trust in the words of God found in the law (4:12), rather than trusting in the words of Satan found in the Antichrist's twisting of scripture (4:7). Chapter 5 warns against following those materially rich people, who have aligned themselves with the Antichrist (5:1-6). Instead, they need to endure tribulation (5:7-11) and help each other through prayer in order to save their souls from death (5:14-20).

Much like Ephesians gives advanced doctrine for those today who already know Romans doctrine, **I Peter** gives advanced doctrine for those in Israel in the tribulation period who already understand Hebrews doctrine. I Peter 1 deals with the blessings they have in Christ, and those blessings come about through the trial of their faith (1:7), making them holy (1:15-16). Chapter 2 shows that they have moved from not being God's people (2:10; Hosea 1:9-11) to being God's "royal priesthood, an holy nation"

(2:9) to reconcile the Gentiles back to God in God's eternal kingdom on earth. Chapter 3 tells the believing remnant of Israel to live godly lives, even though they will suffer persecution for doing so (3:16-17), as did Christ (3:18) and Noah (3:20-21), who is a type of the believing remnant of Israel enduring the tribulation period. Chapter 4 tells Israel to think like Christ did, which means being willing to suffer for Christ's sake. Chapter 5 tells the elders to hold fast to sound doctrine, lest Satan devour the little flock.

II Peter is written to the believing remnant for the last half of the tribulation period, when it will be harder to continue in the faith of Christ. Chapter 1 reminds them to stand on the Word of God. Chapter 2 warns of the false prophets, who will come into the church and try to lead the little flock astray. Chapter 3 puts chapters 1 and 2 together to tell them not to listen to those who doubt the Word of God.

Like Philippians corrects bad, practical application of Ephesians doctrine, I – III John focuses on the love of God that should be seen in the little flock during the tribulation period. **I John** says that, if a man is born again ("Born again" is a term used exclusively for Israel, since they are God's firstborn (Exodus 4:22). Today, in the body of Christ, we are "a new creature" in Christ (II Corinthians 5:17).), he will obey God's law and demonstrate God's love to others. This happens under the new covenant in the kingdom, but the little flock can make the choice to have this happen during the tribulation period as well, so that all of the lost sheep of Israel may be saved. If they have faith in God's provision for them under the law covenant, they will grow up from being children, to being young men, to being fathers in the faith (2:12-14). I John also warns against false prophets and antichrists and says that the little flock will be able to recognize them by comparing what they say with what God says in His Word. **II John** is instruction for the millennial kingdom to both believing Israel under the new covenant and Gentiles, who are to learn God's law during that time. **III John** is instruction to the Gentiles in the millennial kingdom so that they are not deceived by false doctrine and false teachers.

The book of **Jude** is much like II Peter 2 in that it warns the church about not being deceived by unbelievers, who come into the church and pretend to be following God and His Word. They are really "brute beasts" (v. 10), deserving "the blackness of darkness for ever" (v. 13). They are like the devil's angels (v. 6), the people of Sodom and Gomorrah (v. 7), the devil in dealing with Moses (v. 9), Cain (v. 11), Balaam (v. 11), Core (v. 11), and the people of Enoch's day (v. 14). Thus, the little flock has people to compare them to, in order to identify them as "mockers," walking "after their own ungodly lusts" (v. 18) so that the little flock does not get carried away by them.

Much like I & II Thessalonians talks about the hope that we have today in heavenly places, the book of **the Revelation** talks about the hope that Israel has in God's eternal kingdom after the tribulation period is over. Daniel was told to "shut up the words" (Daniel 12:4), regarding the end times, but Revelation reveals those events.

Revelation 1 shows the Lord Jesus Christ as the One Israel can trust in to bring them into the kingdom. Chapters 2-3 give instructions to churches in the tribulation period so that they may endure unto the end and be saved. Chapters 4-5 show the power of the Lord Jesus Christ to bring about the events of the tribulation period in order to refine Israel so that they may become "kings and priests" (5:9-10) in God's eternal kingdom on earth. Chapter 6 gives a summary of the entire 7-year tribulation period. Chapter 7 shows the result of these events will be 144,000 Jews sealed for God (7:1-8) midway through the tribulation period and an innumerable multitude making into God's kingdom at Jesus' second coming (7:9-10). Chapters 8-9 give specific plagues God sends on the earth during the last half of the tribulation period as a response to the prayers of the saints. Chapter 10 goes all the way to the end to show that the Lord Jesus Christ will create a new heaven and a new earth to replace the current ones. Therefore, no one should be concerned about the current earth being messed up by a bunch of plagues.

Chapter 11 tells how God will get 144,000 Jews to be saved, and it is through the ministry of the two witnesses during the first half of the tribulation period. Chapter 12 covers the events from the beginning of Israel's program to the end to show how Satan took the kingdoms of the world temporarily away from man and how God will take them back forever and give them to His Son, the man Christ Jesus. Chapter 13 shows Satan's all-out attack of the believing remnant during the last half of the tribulation period by instituting the mark of the beast and having the Anti-Christ (the beast) and the Anti-Holy Ghost (the false prophet) to form a false trinity with him as Anti-God.

Chapter 14 shows that those, who endure unto the end, will stand with the Lamb in the kingdom, and God gives warnings to the earth through angels just before He destroys the wicked at the end of the tribulation period. Chapters 15-16 give details of the seven, last plagues God pours upon the earth. Chapters 17-18 show the religious (ch. 17) and economic (ch. 18) power, known as Babylon, that is over the world in the last half of the tribulation period, being destroyed by God. Chapter 19 shows Jesus' coming to destroy all those aligned with the Antichrist and to marry the land of Israel. Chapter 20 reveals that God's eternal kingdom on earth is broken into two segments. The first is 1,000 years long, in which Satan is in a bottomless pit (20:2-3). During this time, Israel goes to all the Gentiles with God's law (Matthew 28:19-20). The Gentiles respond by taking hold of the Jews (Zechariah 8:23) and going with them to Zion to learn the law of the Lord and to worship Him there (Isaiah 2:2-3). However, because He rules with a rod of iron and destroys the Gentiles who rebel against Him (Psalm 2:8-12), many Gentiles will not want to be in

God's kingdom. Therefore, when Satan is loosed from the bottomless pit, many Gentiles join forces with him (20:7-8). They are destroyed at that time (20:9-10). Then, all unbelievers from mankind's history are judged and cast into the lake of fire (20:11-15). All that is left, then, are believers. Therefore, God establishes a new heaven and a new earth (21:1). The holy city, new Jerusalem, which is detailed in chapter 21, comes down from heaven (21:2), and Israel, as the Lamb's wife (21:9), dwells with the Lord Jesus Christ on earth forever. Chapter 22 ends the Bible, showing Israel dwelling in God's earthly kingdom forever with no more curse of sin to bother them.

Section II.

Each Bible book summarized in one sentence with its key verse

GENESIS

Summary: Man sins (3:6-7) and gives dominion of the earth to Satan (3:14), and God promises to get it back through the seed of the woman (3:15) coming through Israel (12:1-3).

Key passage: 12:1-3 (1) Now the LORD had said unto Abram, Get thee out of thy country, and from thy kindred, and from thy father's house, unto a land that I will show thee: (2) And I will make of thee a great nation, and I will bless thee, and make thy name great; and thou shalt be a blessing: (3) And I will bless them that bless thee, and curse him that curseth thee: and in thee shall all families of the earth be blessed.

EXODUS

Summary: God saves Israel from Egypt (14:26-30), and they will be priests of God to reconcile the whole earth back to God (19:5-6).

Key passage: 19:5-6 (5) Now therefore, if ye will obey my voice indeed, and keep my covenant, then ye shall be a peculiar treasure unto me above all people: for all the earth is mine: (6) And ye shall be unto me a kingdom of priests, and an holy nation. These are the words which thou shalt speak unto the children of Israel.

LEVITICUS

Summary: God calls Israel to be holy (11:44) by following His commands (26:3-13).

Key passage: 11:44 For I am the LORD your God: ye shall therefore sanctify yourselves, and ye shall be holy; for I am holy: neither shall ye defile yourselves with any manner of creeping thing that creepeth upon the earth.

NUMBERS

Summary: Israel wanders in the wilderness for 40 years (14:33) and does not enter the Promised Land, due to their unbelief (14:11).

Key passage: 14:29-33 (29) Your carcases shall fall in this wilderness; and all that were numbered of you, according to your whole number, from twenty years old and upward, which have murmured against me, (30) Doubtless ye shall not come into the land, concerning which I sware to make you dwell therein, save Caleb the son of Jephunneh, and Joshua the son of Nun. (31) But your little ones, which ye said should be a prey, them will I bring in, and they shall know the land which ye have despised. (32) But as for you, your carcases, they shall fall in this wilderness. (33) And your children shall wander in the wilderness forty years, and bear your whoredoms, until your carcases be wasted in the wilderness.

DEUTERONOMY

Summary: God gives the law to the next generation of Israelites (1:3) for them to obey and enter the Promised Land (1:8).

Key passage: 7:6-11 (6) For thou art an holy people unto the LORD thy God: the LORD thy God hath chosen thee to be a special people unto himself, above all people that are upon the face of the earth. (7) The LORD did not set his love upon you, nor choose you, because ye were more in number than any people; for ye were the fewest of all people: (8) But because the LORD loved you, and because he would keep the oath which he had sworn unto your fathers, hath the LORD brought you out with a mighty hand, and redeemed you out of the house of bondmen, from the hand of Pharaoh king of Egypt. (9) Know therefore that the LORD thy God, he is God, the faithful God, which keepeth covenant and mercy with them that love him and keep his commandments to a thousand generations; (10) And repayeth them that hate him to their face, to destroy them: he will not be slack to him that hateth him, he will repay him to his face. (11) Thou shalt therefore keep the commandments, and the statutes, and the judgments, which I command thee this day, to do them.

JOSHUA

Summary: Israel enters the Promised Land and obeys God.

Key passage: 24:31 And Israel served the LORD all the days of Joshua, and all the days of the elders that overlived Joshua, and which had known all the works of the LORD, that he had done for Israel.

JUDGES

Summary: Israel falls into sin to the point where everyone does what is right in his own eyes, not in God's eyes.

Key passage: 21:25 In those days there was no king in Israel: every man did that which was right in his own eyes.

RUTH

Summary: An Israelite, Boaz, saves a Moabitess, Ruth, by marriage, to picture Jesus Christ's future redemption of all the nations back to God (4:9-12 and Genesis 12:1-3).

Key passage: 1:16 And Ruth said, Entreat me not to leave thee, or to return from following after thee: for whither thou goest, I will go; and where thou lodgest, I will lodge: thy people shall be my people, and thy God my God:

I SAMUEL

Summary: Israel rejects God as their king.

Key passage: 8:5 And said unto him, Behold, thou art old, and thy sons walk not in thy ways: now make us a king to judge us like all the nations.

II SAMUEL

Summary: God makes an everlasting covenant with David as king and his son, Jesus Christ, the seed of the woman.

Key passage: 7:12-16 (12) And when thy days be fulfilled, and thou shalt sleep with thy fathers, I will set up thy seed after thee, which shall proceed out of thy bowels, and I will establish his kingdom. (13) He shall build an house for my name, and I will stablish the throne of his kingdom for ever. (14) I will be his father, and he shall be my son. If he commit iniquity, I will chasten him with the rod of men, and with the stripes of the children of men: (15) But my mercy shall not depart away from him, as I took it from Saul, whom I put away before thee. (16) And thine house and thy kingdom shall be established for ever before thee: thy throne shall be established for ever.

I KINGS

Summary: Israel is divided into two kingdoms—Israel and Judah—and God's people are now just Judah (11:31-37).

Key passage: 11:11-13 (11) Wherefore the LORD said unto Solomon, Forasmuch as this is done of thee, and thou hast not kept my covenant and my statutes, which I have commanded thee, I will surely rend the kingdom from thee, and will give it to thy servant. (12) Notwithstanding in thy days I will not do it for David thy father's sake: but I will rend it out of the hand of thy son.

(13) Howbeit I will not rend away all the kingdom; but will give one tribe to thy son for David my servant's sake, and for Jerusalem's sake which I have chosen.

II KINGS

Summary: Both Israel (17:20-23) and Judah (24) go into 70 years of captivity for failing to believe and obey God's law covenant with them, and the seed of the woman survives another attack by Satan.

Key passage: 11:2-3 (2) But Jehosheba, the daughter of king Joram, sister of Ahaziah, took Joash the son of Ahaziah, and stole him from among the king's sons which were slain; and they hid him, even him and his nurse, in the bedchamber from Athaliah, so that he was not slain. (3) And he was with her hid in the house of the LORD six years. And Athaliah did reign over the land.

I CHRONICLES

Summary: David's servants in Israel are listed (11:10-12:40 & chs. 23-27), as a type of Jesus Christ's servants in God's future, eternal kingdom on earth.

Key passage: 17:9 Also I will ordain a place for my people Israel, and will plant them, and they shall dwell in their place, and shall be moved no more; neither shall the children of wickedness waste them any more, as at the beginning,

II CHRONICLES

Summary: This book gives God's dealings with Judah as they fall into sin, culminating in 70 years of Babylonian captivity (36:20-21).

Key passage: 36:14-21 (14) Moreover all the chief of the priests, and the people, transgressed very much after all the abominations of the heathen; and polluted the house of the LORD which he had hallowed in Jerusalem. (15)

And the LORD God of their fathers sent to them by his messengers, rising up betimes, and sending; because he had compassion on his people, and on his dwelling place: (16) But they mocked the messengers of God, and despised his words, and misused his prophets, until the wrath of the LORD arose against his people, till there was no remedy. (17) Therefore he brought upon them the king of the Chaldees, who slew their young men with the sword in the house of their sanctuary, and had no compassion upon young man or maiden, old man, or him that stooped for age: he gave them all into his hand. (18) And all the vessels of the house of God, great and small, and the treasures of the house of the LORD, and the treasures of the king, and of his princes; all these he brought to Babylon. (19) And they burnt the house of God, and brake down the wall of Jerusalem, and burnt all the palaces thereof with fire, and destroyed all the goodly vessels thereof. (20) And them that had escaped from the sword carried he away to Babylon; where they were servants to him and his sons until the reign of the kingdom of Persia: (21) To fulfil the word of the LORD by the mouth of Jeremiah, until the land had enjoyed her sabbaths: for as long as she lay desolate she kept sabbath, to fulfil threescore and ten years.

EZRA

Summary: Judah returns from captivity and rebuilds the temple in Jerusalem.

Key passage: 1:2-3 (2) Thus saith Cyrus king of Persia, The LORD God of heaven hath given me all the kingdoms of the earth; and he hath charged me to build him an house at Jerusalem, which is in Judah. (3) Who is there among you of all his people? his God be with him, and let him go up to Jerusalem, which is in Judah, and build the house of the LORD God of Israel, (he is the God,) which is in Jerusalem.

NEHEMIAH

Summary: Judah returns from captivity and rebuilds the wall of Jerusalem.

Key passage: 2:17 Then said I unto them, Ye see the distress that we are in, how Jerusalem lieth waste, and the gates thereof are burned with fire: come, and let us build up the wall of Jerusalem, that we be no more a reproach.

ESTHER

Summary: God saves Israel from extinction through Esther and Mordecai, as a type of God saving Israel eternally through the seed of the woman, the Lord Jesus Christ.

Key passage: 4:13-14 (13) Then Mordecai commanded to answer Esther, Think not with thyself that thou shalt escape in the king's house, more than all the Jews. (14) For if thou altogether holdest thy peace at this time, then shall there enlargement and deliverance arise to the Jews from another place; but thou and thy father's house shall be destroyed: and who knoweth whether thou art come to the kingdom for such a time as this?

JOB

Summary: Job loses his riches (1:14-19), goes through trials (2:7-25:6), and receives more riches in the end than he had at the beginning (42:10), as a type of Israel losing the kingdom, going through the tribulation period, and receiving more in God's earthly, eternal kingdom.

Key passage: 1:21 And said, Naked came I out of my mother's womb, and naked shall I return thither: the LORD gave, and the LORD hath taken away; blessed be the name of the LORD.

PSALMS

Summary: The Psalms are songs that depict Israel's entire history with Jesus Christ at the center, saving them through His death and bringing them into God's eternal, earthly kingdom to reign with Him.

Key passage: 138:2 I will worship toward thy holy temple, and praise thy name for thy lovingkindness and for thy truth: for thou hast magnified thy word above all thy name.

PROVERBS

Summary: The foolish woman of religion and the wise woman of God's commandments compete for Israel's affections through the tribulation period, culminating in a believing remnant of Israel choosing the wise woman.

Key passage: 1:7 The fear of the LORD is the beginning of knowledge: but fools despise wisdom and instruction.

ECCLESIASTES

Summary: God shows Israel the vanity of worldly wisdom (1:2) so that they will learn to "fear God: and keep His commandments" (12:13).

Key passage: 8:11-12 (11) Because sentence against an evil work is not executed speedily, therefore the heart of the sons of men is fully set in them to do evil. (12) Though a sinner do evil an hundred times, and his days be prolonged, yet surely I know that it shall be well with them that fear God, which fear before him:

SONG OF SOLOMON

Summary: The song is a love story of Christ and Israel, and they will be united in marriage at Jesus' second coming.

Key passage: 2:16 My beloved is mine, and I am his: he feedeth among the lilies.

ISAIAH

Summary: God's redemption of Israel from being Satan's lawful captive (49:24-25) is seen in Jesus Christ being cut off from the land of the living for Israel's transgressions (53:8).

Key passage: 7:14 Therefore the Lord himself shall give you a sign; Behold, a virgin shall conceive, and bear a son, and shall call his name Immanuel.

JEREMIAH

Summary: ISRAEL (not us today) is so steeped in sin that only God can save her, which He will do by making a new covenant with her through Christ's death (31:31-34).

Key passage: 11:13-14 (13) For according to the number of thy cities were thy gods, O Judah; and according to the number of the streets of Jerusalem have ye set up altars to that shameful thing, even altars to burn incense unto Baal. (14) Therefore pray not thou for this people, neither lift up a cry or prayer for them: for I will not hear them in the time that they cry unto me for their trouble.

LAMENTATIONS

Summary: The believing remnant of Israel weeps over their captivity, but they take comfort in knowing that God remains faithful to them, even when they have played the harlot.

Key passage: 3:22-23 (22) It is of the LORD'S mercies that we are not consumed, because his compassions fail not. (23) They are new every morning: great is thy faithfulness.

EZEKIEL

Summary: God leaves the temple and Jerusalem (8:4-11:25) because of Israel's uncleanness, but God will cleanse ISRAEL (not us today) and make them a virgin, fit for marrying God's Son under the new covenant (36:22-32).

Key passage: 36:24-28 (24) For I will take you from among the heathen, and gather you out of all countries, and will bring you into your own land. (25) Then will I sprinkle clean water upon you, and ye shall be clean: from all your filthiness, and from all your idols, will I cleanse you. (26) A new heart also will I give you, and a new spirit will I put within you: and I will take away the stony heart out of your flesh, and I will give you an heart of flesh. (27) And I will put my spirit within you, and cause you to walk in my statutes, and ye shall keep my judgments, and do them. (28) And ye shall dwell in the land that I gave to your fathers; and ye shall be my people, and I will be your God.

DANIEL

Summary: The believing remnant of Judah is protected by God in captivity (3:19-28 and 6:16-22), as a type of them going through the tribulation period, while even Satan, through the Antichrist (11:36-45), is powerless to stop God from making an end of sins (9:24-27) and bringing in God's eternal kingdom on earth (2:44).

Key passage: 9:24-27 (24) Seventy weeks are determined upon thy people and upon thy holy city, to finish the transgression, and to make an end of sins, and to make reconciliation for iniquity, and to bring in everlasting righteousness, and to seal up the vision and prophecy, and to anoint the most Holy. (25) Know therefore and understand, that from the going forth of the commandment to restore and to build Jerusalem unto the Messiah the Prince shall be seven weeks, and threescore and two weeks: the street shall be built again, and the wall, even in troublous times. (26) And after threescore and two weeks shall Messiah be cut off, but not for himself: and the people of the prince that shall come shall destroy the city and the sanctuary; and the end thereof shall be with a flood, and unto the end of the war desolations are determined. (27) And he shall confirm the covenant with many for one week: and in the midst of the week he shall cause the sacrifice and the oblation to cease, and for the overspreading of abominations he shall make it desolate, even until the consummation, and that determined shall be poured upon the desolate.

HOSEA

Summary: Hosea marries a prostitute (1:1-3) and has a child that is not God's (1:9), as a picture of Israel playing the harlot with Satan and not being God's people from the time of Paul's call in Acts 9 until the future catching away of the body of Christ.

Key passage: 1:9-10 (9) Then said God, Call his name Loammi: for ye are not my people, and I will not be your God. (10) Yet the number of the children of Israel shall be as the sand of the sea, which cannot be measured nor numbered; and it shall come to pass, that in the place where it was said unto them, Ye are not my people, there it shall be said unto them, Ye are the sons of the living God.

JOEL

Summary: The time is here for Israel to fast and mourn with godly sorrow over their sins (2:12-17) so that God may pour His Spirit upon them in the last days (2:28-29).

Key passage: 2:30-32 (30) And I will show wonders in the heavens and in the earth, blood, and fire, and pillars of smoke. (31) The sun shall be turned into darkness, and the moon into blood, before the great and the terrible day of the LORD come. (32) And it shall come to pass, that whosoever shall call on the name of the LORD shall be delivered: for in mount Zion and in Jerusalem shall be deliverance, as the LORD hath said, and in the remnant whom the LORD shall call.

AMOS

Summary: God's wrath is poured out on all nations, including Israel and Judah (chs. 1:1-9:10), including a 400-year famine from hearing God's Word (8:11-12), but God will restore Israel in the end (9:11-15).

Key passage: 8:11-12 (11) Behold, the days come, saith the Lord GOD, that I will send a famine in the land, not a famine of bread, nor a thirst for water, but of hearing the words of the LORD: (12) And they shall wander from sea to sea, and from the north even to the east, they shall run to and fro to seek the word of the LORD, and shall not find it.

OBADIAH

Summary: God pours His wrath upon Edom for their sins (1-14), which shows Israel that God will do the same to them (15-16), if they do not obey God's law covenant with them.

Key passage: 21 And saviours shall come up on mount Zion to judge the mount of Esau; and the kingdom shall be the LORD'S.

JONAH

Summary: God saves wicked Nineveh (3:10), which shows Israel that He wants to do the same for them, if they will just have faith in God's law covenant with them.

Key passage: 3:10 And God saw their works, that they turned from their evil way; and God repented of the evil, that he had said that he would do unto them; and he did it not.

MICAH

Summary: God will destroy the idolatry and false religion of Israel (1:2-7) and establish His kingdom in Jerusalem with all nations coming to worship God there (4:1-5).

Key passage: 4:1-2 (1) But in the last days it shall come to pass, that the mountain of the house of the LORD shall be established in the top of the mountains, and it shall be exalted above the hills; and people shall flow unto it. (2) And many nations shall come, and say, Come, and let us go up to the mountain of the LORD, and to the house of the God of Jacob; and he will teach us of his ways, and we will walk in his paths: for the law shall go forth of Zion, and the word of the LORD from Jerusalem.

NAHUM

Summary: God destroys Nineveh for their wickedness, showing Israel that they will not be spared God's judgment by trusting in past righteousness found in Israel.

Key passage: 1:15 Behold upon the mountains the feet of him that bringeth good tidings, that publisheth peace! O Judah, keep thy solemn feasts, perform thy vows: for the wicked shall no more pass through thee; he is utterly cut off.

HABAKKUK

Summary: The believing remnant of Israel cries for God's justice in the midst of a wicked nation (1:12-17), but they will continue to trust in God, because "the just shall live by his faith" (2:4).

Key passage: 2:4 Behold, his soul which is lifted up is not upright in him: but the just shall live by his faith.

ZEPHANIAH

Summary: God is ready to destroy all that is in Jerusalem, so that He can bring in His believing remnant and set up His eternal kingdom on earth in Jerusalem (1:14-18).

Key passage: 1:14-17 (14) The great day of the LORD is near, it is near, and hasteth greatly, even the voice of the day of the LORD: the mighty man shall cry there bitterly. (15) That day is a day of wrath, a day of trouble and distress, a day of wasteness and desolation, a day of darkness and gloominess, a day of clouds and thick darkness, (16) A day of the trumpet and alarm against the fenced cities, and against the high towers. (17) And I will bring distress upon men, that they shall walk like blind men, because they have sinned against the LORD: and their blood shall be poured out as dust, and their flesh as the dung.

HAGGAI

Summary: The beginning of a believing remnant of Israel coming back from captivity is seen here (2:1-5), and God will build the little flock into the Israel of God that will enter the kingdom (2:6-9).

Key passage: 2:9 The glory of this latter house shall be greater than of the former, saith the LORD of hosts: and in this place will I give peace, saith the LORD of hosts.

ZECHARIAH

Summary: The Christ will be God's servant to build the Israel of God (3:8-10, 6:12-13), and then He will come in power to destroy the wicked (14) and bring the righteous into the kingdom (10:10-12).

Key passage: 6:12-13 (12) And speak unto him, saying, Thus speaketh the LORD of hosts, saying, Behold the man whose name is The BRANCH; and he shall grow up out of his place, and he shall build the temple of the LORD: (13) Even he shall build the temple of the LORD; and he shall bear the glory, and shall sit and rule upon his throne; and he shall be a priest upon his throne: and the counsel of peace shall be between them both.

MALACHI

Summary: God hates Israel's religion (1:12-14) and will destroy it with His messenger preparing the way (3:1), the tribulation period (3:2-4), and Elijah (4:5-6).

Key passage: 3:1-4 (1) Behold, I will send my messenger, and he shall prepare the way before me: and the Lord, whom ye seek, shall suddenly come to his temple, even the messenger of the covenant, whom ye delight in: behold, he shall come, saith the LORD of hosts. (2) But who may abide the day of his coming? and who shall stand when he appeareth? for he is like a refiner's fire, and like fullers' soap: (3) And he shall sit as a refiner and purifier of silver: and he shall purify the sons of Levi, and purge them as gold and silver, that they may offer unto the LORD an offering in righteousness. (4) Then shall the offering of Judah and Jerusalem be pleasant unto the LORD, as in the days of old, and as in former years.

MATTHEW

Summary: The Christ comes as Israel's king (2:2), binds Satan through His death, burial, and resurrection (12:29), and now has the power to bring Israel into the kingdom (28:18).

Key passage: 28:18 And Jesus came and spake unto them, saying, All power is given unto me in heaven and in earth.

MARK

Summary: The Christ comes as Israel's servant, taking their sin payment through His death, and preparing them to enter the kingdom through physical miracles.

Key passage: 15:34 & 16:6 (34) And at the ninth hour Jesus cried with a loud voice, saying, Eloi, Eloi, lama sabachthani? which is, being interpreted, My God, my God, why hast thou forsaken me? (6) And he saith unto them, Be not affrighted: Ye seek Jesus of Nazareth, which was crucified: he is risen; he is not here: behold the place where they laid him.

LUKE

Summary: The Christ comes as Israel's man, living a sinless life and dying as her kinsmen redeemer, while also performing physical miracles to demonstrate the spiritual healing (forgiveness of sins) that God wants to give them to bring them into the kingdom.

Key passage: 13:6-9 (6) He spake also this parable; A certain man had a fig tree planted in his vineyard; and he came and sought fruit thereon, and found none. (7) Then said he unto the dresser of his vineyard, Behold, these three years I come seeking fruit on this fig tree, and find none: cut it down; why cumbereth it the ground? (8) And he answering said unto him, Lord, let it alone this year also, till I shall dig about it, and dung it: (9) And if it bear fruit, well: and if not, then after that thou shalt cut it down.

JOHN

Summary: The Christ comes as Israel's God, making sure Christ Jesus, the man, fulfills all the requirements necessary to bring eternal life to all people who believe what God tells them.

Key passage: 20:30-31 (30) And many other signs truly did Jesus in the presence of his disciples, which are not written in this book: (31) But these are written, that ye might believe that Jesus is the Christ, the Son of God; and that believing ye might have life through his name.

ACTS

Summary: The at-hand phase of the kingdom goes away due to Israel's unbelief (7:55-56), and God begins reconciling the heavenly places back to Himself by saving Paul and all those who believe his gospel (Romans 16:25).

Key passage: 7:55 But he, being full of the Holy Ghost, looked up stedfastly into heaven, and saw the glory of God, and Jesus standing on the right hand of God,

ROMANS

Summary: Romans begins the section that is written to us today, and it explains that the cross means that we can have justification (3:21-31) and live in Christ (chs. 6-8) right now (5:9,11) by faith in Jesus' death, burial, and resurrection.

Key passage: 3:21-25 (21) But now the righteousness of God without the law is manifested, being witnessed by the law and the prophets; (22) Even the righteousness of God which is by faith of Jesus Christ unto all and upon all them that believe: for there is no difference: (23) For all have sinned, and come short of the glory of God; (24) Being justified freely by his grace through the redemption that is in Christ Jesus: (25) Whom God hath set forth to be a propitiation through faith in his blood, to declare his righteousness for the remission of sins that are past, through the forbearance of God;

I CORINTHIANS

Summary: This book is written to correct the carnal lifestyles (3:1-4) of the Corinthians, because they do not have faith in the Romans doctrine of salvation and sanctification by the cross work of Christ (15:1-4).

Key passage: 15:16-20 (16) For if the dead rise not, then is not Christ raised: (17) And if Christ be not raised, your faith is vain; ye are yet in your sins. (18) Then they also which are fallen asleep in Christ are perished. (19) If in this life only we have hope in Christ, we are of all men most miserable. (20) But now is Christ risen from the dead, and become the firstfruits of them that slept.

II CORINTHIANS

Summary: The Corinthians need to recognize that suffering for the believer is part of God's plan (4:7-5:8), and Satan tries to trick them into believing otherwise (4:1-4) by having Satan's ministers appear to represent Christ (11:13-15).

Key passage: 12:9-10 (9) And he said unto me, My grace is sufficient for thee: for my strength is made perfect in weakness. Most gladly therefore will I rather glory in my infirmities, that the power of Christ may rest upon me. (10) Therefore I take pleasure in infirmities, in reproaches, in necessities, in persecutions, in distresses for Christ's sake: for when I am weak, then am I strong.

GALATIANS

Summary: Believing that we are crucified and raised with Christ (2:19-21) is essential to walking in the Spirit (5:16) so as to get rid of legalism (6:12) and stand fast in the liberty we have in Christ (5:1-2).

Key passage: 2:19-21 (19) For I through the law am dead to the law, that I might live unto God. (20) I am crucified with Christ: nevertheless I live; yet not I, but Christ liveth in me: and the life which I now live in the flesh I live by the faith of the Son of God, who loved me, and gave himself for me. (21) I do not frustrate the grace of God: for if righteousness come by the law, then Christ is dead in vain.

EPHESIANS

Summary: Christ will fill the heavenly places with the body of Christ (1:18-23), and they should live as if they are already there (5:1-10), because, as far as God is concerned, they are there right now (2:5-6).

Key passage: 2:5-6 (5) Even when we were dead in sins, hath quickened us together with Christ, (by grace ye are saved;) (6) And hath raised us up together, and made us sit together in heavenly places in Christ Jesus:

PHILIPPIANS

Summary: Being in heavenly places in Christ (3:20-21), the Philippians should count the things of this world as dung (3:8) and seek to know Christ in his sufferings (3:10) for the edification of the body of Christ (1:24) and for the soul salvation of unbelievers (4:22).

Key passage: 1:21-22 (21) For to me to live is Christ, and to die is gain. (22) But if I live in the flesh, this is the fruit of my labour: yet what I shall choose I wot not.

COLOSSIANS

Summary: The Colossians should set their affections on things above (3:2), so that they set aside man's religion (2:16-23) and works of the flesh (3:5-9) and hold to the sound doctrine of heavenly places found in Ephesians.

Key passage: 3:2-3 (2) Set your affection on things above, not on things on the earth. (3) For ye are dead, and your life is hid with Christ in God.

I THESSALONIANS

Summary: This epistle gives the body of Christ the sound doctrine of the hope we have in heaven (4:13-18), along with exhortations to continue to live out Romans and Ephesians doctrine (5:16-22).

Key passage: 4:16-18 (16) For the Lord himself shall descend from heaven with a shout, with the voice of the archangel, and with the trump of God: and the dead in Christ shall rise first: (17) Then we which are alive and remain shall be caught up together with them in the clouds, to meet the Lord in the air: and so shall we ever be with the Lord. (18) Wherefore comfort one another with these words.

II THESSALONIANS

Summary: This is another epistle to get their focus on the hope they have in heaven (2:1-2), and it also covers how to deal with busybodies and those in their midst not following sound doctrine (3:6-15).

Key passage: 2:7-8 (7) For the mystery of iniquity doth already work: only he who now letteth will let, until he be taken out of the way. (8) And then shall that Wicked be revealed, whom the Lord shall consume with the spirit of his mouth, and shall destroy with the brightness of his coming:

I TIMOTHY

Summary: This epistle deals with keeping false doctrine out of the church (1 and 6:3-10), gives qualifications for church leaders (3), and deals with church order (2:8-15 and 5).

Key passage: 2:4-6 (4) Who will have all men to be saved, and to come unto the knowledge of the truth. (5) For there is one God, and one mediator between God and men, the man Christ Jesus; (6) Who gave himself a ransom for all, to be testified in due time.

II TIMOTHY

Summary: This epistle gives encouragement to church bishops to stay true to sound doctrine and keep false doctrine out of the church at all costs (1-2), even though many will go astray (1:15, 3, and 4:10-16) as we get closer to being caught up to meet Christ in the air to forever be with the Lord (I Thessalonians 4:17).

Key passage: 2:15-16 (15) Study to show thyself approved unto God, a workman that needeth not to be ashamed, rightly dividing the word of truth. (16) But shun profane and vain babblings: for they will increase unto more ungodliness.

TITUS

Summary: This church epistle covers the expected spiritual maturity level of each person in the church (2), while exhorting Titus to keep false doctrine out of the church (1:10-16).

Key passage: 2:12-14 (12) Teaching us that, denying ungodliness and worldly lusts, we should live soberly, righteously, and godly, in this present world; (13) Looking for that blessed hope, and the glorious appearing of the great God and our Saviour Jesus Christ; (14) Who gave himself for us, that he might redeem us from all iniquity, and purify unto himself a peculiar people, zealous of good works.

PHILEMON

Summary: Onesimus serves as an example of how sound doctrine can change someone from being a no-good unbeliever to being a believer, profitable to building "an holy temple in the Lord" (Ephesians 2:21).

Key passage: 6-7 (6) That the communication of thy faith may become effectual by the acknowledging of every good thing which is in you in Christ Jesus. (7) For we have great joy and consolation in thy love, because the bowels of the saints are refreshed by thee, brother.

HEBREWS

Summary: Hebrews begins the last section of the Bible, which covers Israel in the tribulation period; it shows the HEBREWS (not us today) that they have a second chance to be in God's earthly kingdom thanks to the cross work of Christ, but Israel must have faith in God in order to enter the kingdom.

Key passage: 9:15 And for this cause he is the mediator of the new testament, that by means of death, for the redemption of the transgressions that were under the first testament, they which are called might receive the promise of eternal inheritance.

JAMES

Summary: James encourages the little flock of Israel to endure unto the end of the tribulation period (Matthew 24:13) with faith plus works in line with that faith (2:17-26).

Key passage: 2:24 Ye see then how that by works a man is justified, and not by faith only.

I PETER

Summary: Israel is encouraged to endure the tribulation period so that they may fulfill their calling of being God's priests to the Gentiles in God's eternal kingdom on earth (2:5-10).

Key passage: 2:9-10 (9) But ye are a chosen generation, a royal priesthood, an holy nation, a peculiar people; that ye should show forth the praises of him who hath called you out of darkness into his marvellous light: (10) Which in time past were not a people, but are now the people of God: which had not obtained mercy, but now have obtained mercy.

II PETER

Summary: The little flock of Israel needs to beware of false prophets and teachers, who will try to come in and devour the flock (2), and keep their trust in the second coming of Christ to save them (3:9-14).

Key passage: 3:9 The Lord is not slack concerning his promise, as some men count slackness; but is longsuffering to us-ward, not willing that any should perish, but that all should come to repentance.

I JOHN

Summary: This epistle concentrates on the love of God that will be shown by the little flock to the lost sheep of Israel, when the little flock obeys God's commandments.

Key passage: 5:7-9 (7) For there are three that bear record in heaven, the Father, the Word, and the Holy Ghost: and these three are one. (8) And there are three that bear witness in earth, the Spirit, and the water, and the blood: and these three agree in one. (9) If we receive the witness of men, the witness of God is greater: for this is the witness of God which he hath testified of his Son.

II JOHN

Summary: This epistle gives encouragement to believing Israel in the millennial kingdom to reach all Gentiles with the Mosaic law, and it gives instruction to Gentiles to believe what Israel teaches them during this time.

Key passage: 10-11 (10) If there come any unto you, and bring not this doctrine, receive him not into your house, neither bid him God speed: (11) For he that biddeth him God speed is partaker of his evil deeds.

III JOHN

Summary: This epistle is a warning to Gentile believers in the millennial reign not to listen to false doctrine so that they are not deceived.

Key passage: 4 I have no greater joy than to hear that my children walk in truth.

JUDE

Summary: This epistle warns the little flock of the great opposition within the little flock during the tribulation period, but the Lord Jesus Christ is able to bring them into God's kingdom, in spite of this opposition (24-25).

Key passage: 14-15 (14) And Enoch also, the seventh from Adam, prophesied of these, saying, Behold, the Lord cometh with ten thousands of his saints, (15) To execute judgment upon all, and to convince all that are ungodly among them of all their ungodly deeds which they have ungodly committed, and of all their hard speeches which ungodly sinners have spoken against him.

REVELATION

Summary: Revelation gives details of end-time events that will refine Israel so that they are saved and live forever in God's eternal kingdom on earth.

Key passage: 21:3-4 (3) And I heard a great voice out of heaven saying, Behold, the tabernacle of God is with men, and he will dwell with them, and they shall be his people, and God himself shall be with them, and be their God. (4) And God shall wipe away all tears from their eyes; and there shall be no more death, neither sorrow, nor crying, neither shall there be any more pain: for the former things are passed away.

Made in United States
Troutdale, OR
01/02/2025